The
# CAREGIVER'S
# ESSENTIAL
# HANDBOOK

*More than 1,200 Tips to Help You Care for
and Comfort the Seniors in Your Life*

ɔ Sasha Carr, M.S.,
and Sandra Choron

## Contemporary Books

*Chicago   New York   San Francisco   Lisbon   London   Madrid   Mexico City
Milan   New Delhi   San Juan   Seoul   Singapore   Sydney   Toronto*

Property of Library
Cape Fear Comm College
Wilmington, N. C.

W9-AHU-270

The *McGraw·Hill* Companies

**Library of Congress Cataloging-in-Publication Data**

Choron, Sandra.
    The caregiver's essential handbook : more than 1,200 tips to help you care for and comfort the seniors in your life / Sandra Choron and Sasha Carr.
        p.    cm.
    Includes bibliographical references and index.
    ISBN 0-07-139519-9
        1. Aged—Care—Handbooks, manuals, etc.    2. Caregivers—United States—Handbooks, manuals, etc.    I. Title: The caregiver's essential handbook.    II. Title: The caregiver's essential handbook.    III. Carr, Sandra.    IV. Title.

    HV1451 .C4517    2003
    649.8—dc21                                          2002031414

Copyright © 2003 by Sasha Carr and Sandra Choron. All rights reserved. Printed in the United States of America. Except as permitted under the United States Copyright Act of 1976, no part of this publication may be reproduced or distributed in any form or by any means, or stored in a database or retrieval system, without the prior written permission of the publisher.

1 2 3 4 5 6 7 8 9 0    AGM/AGM    2 1 0 9 8 7 6 5 4 3

ISBN 0-07-139519-9

Interior design by Susan H. Hartman

McGraw-Hill books are available at special quantity discounts to use as premiums and sales promotions, or for use in corporate training programs. For more information, please write to the Director of Special Sales, Professional Publishing, McGraw-Hill, Two Penn Plaza, New York, NY 10121-2298. Or contact your local bookstore.

**Disclaimer**

The purpose of this book is to educate. It is sold with the understanding that the authors and publisher shall have neither liability nor responsibility for any injury caused or alleged to be caused directly or indirectly by the information contained in this book. While every effort has been made to ensure its accuracy, the book's contents should not be construed as medical advice. Each person's health needs are unique. To obtain recommendations appropriate to your particular situation, please consult a qualified health care provider.

This book is printed on acid-free paper.

For my sister, Shirley Glickman, who shows me the way.
—*Sandra Choron*

∾

To Harold Fitzgeorge, for—among countless other things—
deciding I was never "too big" to call him Pop Pop.
—*Sasha Carr*

# Contents

∾

---

## Part III ■ People Who Need People

# Preface

❦

The best books, they say, are born of necessity. . . .

Several years ago, we joined a club: we each became one of the millions of Americans who care for an aging or seriously ill loved one. For Sandy, this meant helping to care for an aging mother through a stroke and a gradual physical and mental decline, while Sasha helped care for her seriously ill sister. We were lucky, though—we had help, but not from the books we first turned to. Some of these were useful; we learned about strokes, heart attacks, and medical procedures from comprehensive texts on the subject. We also obtained lots of information about many of our options regarding medications from some of the hundreds of websites on the subject.

But after tending to our loved ones' immediate needs; dealing with doctors, hospitals, and residences; managing insurance and other financial issues; and coping with all the other practical details that needed to be addressed, neither of us could have imagined having the time to read a four-hundred-page book about caregiving, no matter how helpful it might have been! The real help—knowing what to do when Mom's memory loss threw her into a deep depression, dealing with difficult hospital staff, simplifying the complicated processes of dressing and grooming, finding ways to make life good and safe again when it seemed that so much was lost—came from the only *real* experts we could look to: other experienced caregivers. It seemed that everywhere we turned, we met people who had tips to guide us.

The wisdom gleaned from speaking with others was of tremendous help to each of us personally and was the inspiration for this book. We wanted to put together an easy-to-read collection of truly practical and useful time-tested tips, ingenious solutions, and clever hints to simplify life as a caregiver provided by the *real* experts: others who had been through the process themselves. In researching the book, we spoke with many family caregivers and professional caregivers—nurses, nursing home staff, home health care aides, companions—all with unique experiences and different viewpoints. We also learned a great deal from seniors themselves, who are, after all, firsthand experts on growing older who can teach us a lot. Thus this book also includes important messages that our seniors would like to share with us.

Because of the range of experiences represented in this book, no single reader will need all the tips we have included, so don't try to absorb this entire book. Keep it with you, and browse through it when you're looking for answers, advice, and an understanding voice. Not all of us, for instance, will wind up at the sickbed of someone we love. Many seniors are vital today. It is not uncommon to hear that a middle-aged daughter lives some four hundred miles away from her eighty-three-year-old mother who still swims two times a week. But even she might need ways in which she can gauge her mother's needs more closely as they change. The fact is, none of us really know when and by whom we may be called on.

Each of the "experts" we learned from will tell you that the frustrations and difficulties caregivers endure are many. But just as there seems to be no end to the problems that arise in caregiving, you'll be relieved to find there is also a limitless supply of resources, advice, and wisdom available to you. Whether you're in need of phone numbers and addresses or practical solutions and emotional reassurance, the helpful tips and lifesaving resources offered here will help you plan, manage, and sustain a positive caregiving experience for you and your loved one.

# Acknowledgments

∿

We're grateful to the many seniors, their caregivers, their families, and the professionals who work with them who participated in the lively exchange that made this book possible. The staff and seniors of RP7 at the Hebrew Home for the Aged in Riverdale, New York, and at University Behavioral Healthcare—UMDNJ—made contributions to this book of which they are probably not even aware.

For their support and ideas, we extend special thanks to: Olivia Bayer, Nora Braun, Toni Brown, Stacey Cahn, Ph.D., Barbara Carr, Patrick Carr, Casey and Harry Choron, Tracy Dennis, Ph.D., Roberta Fitzgeorge, Shannon Garrahan, Renee Glick, Lara Glickman, Inez Gordon, Stacy Grossman, Rose Haas, George Hermalyn, Rabbi Simon Hirschhorn, Lee Hyer, Ed.D., Rav Ioja, Maureen Johnson, Lilah Korte, Leigh Lee, Emy Leeser, Ilyse Lesser, L.C.S.W., Susan Levy, Dave Marsh, Mary Marsh, Julia McCormack, Petra Melcher, Audrey Meyers, Alan Novich, C.I.P., Michael O. Palmer, Sheila Pasternak, Kathy Popino, Gail and Moshe Rosenberg, Shoshanna Rosenzweig, Bill Shanahan, Steven Sohnle, Psy.D., Kayleen Sutherland, the Swymer Family, Kim and Josh Targoff, Chris Tingue, Vanya Vargas, Miriam Weinberg, Jenny White, Jenny "Mommy" Wilson, Chris Wright, Dr. Charles Wuhl, and Kim Yuen.

Our editors at Contemporary Books, Matthew Carnicelli and Anthony Sarchiapone, took special interest in this project, and the book would not have been possible without them. We're sincerely grateful to them for their help and good cheer throughout.

Finally, we express our love and gratitude to the memories of Kristen Carr and Fay Samelson, who gave us the inspiration for this book.

PART I

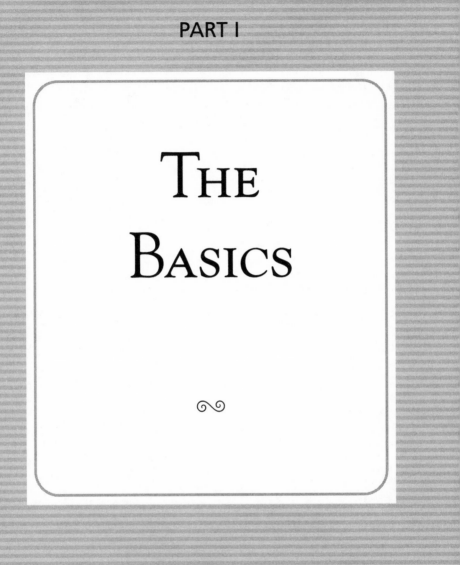

# THE

# BASICS

# Getting Started

∾

## WHERE TO BEGIN?

It's time to start thinking of yourself as a caregiver when the following types of events occur:

- A major health problem, or a collection of smaller ones, is starting to cramp your mother's style.
- Financial problems (overdrawn checks, unpaid bills, huge credit balances) start cropping up.
- Grandpa doesn't get out as much as he used to and seems less interested in what's going on around him.
- Home maintenance is slipping: things that break around the house are not repaired.
- The lawn or garden, once meticulous, becomes overgrown.
- Dad's refrigerator is poorly stocked, or food that is past its prime still hangs around.
- Your grandfather just passed away, and your grandmother is living alone for the first time in forty years.
- Your father doesn't dress as spiffily as he used to and has stopped shaving and doing other personal care rituals.

- Mom has a fender bender at the mall for the second time this year.
- Dad seems distracted or forgetful when you speak to him on the phone.
- You've figured out that helping the senior in your life now, even when there are no clear problems, might help prevent trouble later.

Get online if you're not there already. There is a wealth of helpful information for seniors and caregivers on the Internet. (See Resources at the back of this book for a list of sites that we recommend.) If you can introduce your parents to the Internet, that's great. If you can't, let them watch as you surf just so they can get a feel for the help that's out there. If you're not computer literate or you don't own a computer, go to the library and arrange to take lessons if you can—most public libraries offer Internet access these days. Don't cut yourself off from the world of help that's out there for you.

Don't storm the gates at the first sign of trouble. If you feel you should get more involved in your mother's life, do it as gradually and respectfully as possible. Remember that if you're really trying to help, you'll do a lot better if you don't alienate or overwhelm her.

∾

"It took me a while to realize that my parents needed help. I was so close to the situation and it happened so gradually that I didn't catch on—or maybe I didn't want to catch on and admit that they were in trouble, because it was painful to see. Anyway, my best friend came with me to visit them one afternoon. Since she was more removed and not personally involved, she could see what was going on more clearly, and she opened my eyes to the fact that I needed to take some action."

—*Louise Grady*

Define your responsibilities as a caregiver. Make a list. Set up guidelines for what you will and won't do. Put it in writing and stick to it. If other family members can't help, make a decision to hire someone to perform the duties you can't or would rather not handle.

Make sure your senior joins AARP (formerly the American Association of Retired Persons). Anyone age fifty or older is eligible. For $12.50 a year, members get tons of discounts on everything from prescriptions to travel, plus a subscription to the AARP magazine *Modern Maturity*. Call 1-800-424-3410 or visit aarp.org. (And if *you* are fifty or older, why not join, too?)

Although many seniors programs are federally funded, the best way to contact them is through your local Area Agency on Aging. There is one in your community, even if you're not aware of it. These offices will connect you with a host of services available in your area, including transportation, senior day care programs, senior residences, meal delivery, home care, legal assistance, and just about anything else you can think of (and plenty that you haven't!). You can locate your local agency by calling 1-800-677-1116 or visiting n4a.org.

Get your father hooked into the local senior center. These centers provide transportation services, classes, information, recreation, and the chance to make new friends. Offer to go with him the first few times to help put him at ease.

It's not all-or-nothing. Even if you are not making regular use of the local senior center, people there are still available to answer questions or provide resources. And if your senior only wants to visit the center occasionally, even if it's just for lunch, you're still welcome there.

If your mother is too young (or young at heart) to feel that she needs a senior center's services, a senior center would probably love her help as a volunteer. That way she'll already have a connection to the center further along the line when she starts to need help.

▸ Introduce all new changes in your parents' lives as positives: "Now you won't have to worry about weeding the garden" or "You'll be able to get so much more done now that Jenny is taking care of the cooking."

▸ Don't order; instead, ask. Bad idea: "The house is a wreck! I'm coming over tomorrow to set things straight!" Better idea: "It seems like one or two things need fixing. Would tomorrow be a good time for me to come over and help you take care of them?"

▸ Whenever considering any programs, groups, or services for your mother, check them out on your own first. If a particular place or service doesn't seem right for Mom, you can avoid having one bad experience turn her off.

▸ Make contact with a competent geriatric caseworker. You can contact such professionals through local senior centers or your doctor. Geriatric caseworkers are specially trained to deal with everything from financial and insurance issues to home health care, day care facilities, and volunteer groups that can help you. They're also able to evaluate what your senior's specific needs are. A geriatric caseworker will be an invaluable resource for you; no wonder this is one of the fastest-growing areas of social work.

▸ Make sure your loved one is receiving all the medical and financial benefits available to him. Communicate with providers often to keep them updated and let them know that your loved one is not easy prey for the bureaucracy—he has you on his side!

▸ If your parent served in the military, the Department of Veterans Affairs provides a host of resources, including primary medical care, hospitalization, mental health services, home health care, and nursing home care. But your loved one must first enroll! For more information about benefits, contact your local veterans office. Look under "Government Offices—Veterans Affairs" in the Yellow Pages.

▶ Don't let yourself get overwhelmed by anything—transportation issues, meals, even household chores—without first checking with your local church or other religious or community groups, which often provide these services for the elderly. There are good souls out there—angels, actually!—who want to help. Let them.

▶ Know your neighborhood options: senior day programs, home health aides, assisted living, group living, senior foster care, temporary nursing home care, and so forth. Network! Network! Network!

▶ Give yourself recognition for what you do.

☙

"Somehow, I had lost track of how quickly time was passing. Over the years, I helped make the adjustments in their lives when they were needed—I bought blouses with Velcro closures for Mom when her arthritis got the best of her, and I taught Dad to use the Internet so he could maintain his old interests and even develop new ones. But it wasn't until they both wound up with minor injuries after a car accident that I realized how much they relied on me. I was overwhelmed by the responsibility at first, but when I took stock of the situation and realized that I was now a caregiver—which sounded like someone who walks around in a white uniform and squeaky shoes—then I was able to organize the tasks and make the adjustments in my life that would be necessary for me to do the job well. None of it was easy, but now I'm proud to add 'caregiver' to all the other things I've accomplished in my life."

—*Renee Gerber*

You can accomplish a lot over the phone—but you have to be willing to spend half a day on hold. Be patient! The hold time might go by faster if you fortify yourself with a good book, a crossword puzzle, or some knitting.

Find out if you are eligible for any sort of free or reimbursed home (or other respite) care, whether it's a nursing service or companionship just for a few hours a week. These services must be prescribed by a physician if they are to be reimbursed. If the doctor doesn't suggest this sort of care, don't be shy about raising the subject. He may not be aware of your senior's day-to-day situation.

Keep everyone in the family informed as to how your loved ones are getting along. The earlier you involve family members in their care, the more involved and motivated everyone will feel. Even if it's easier for you to do something yourself than it is to suffer through phone calls with relatives you may not get along with, take the time (and patience) to make the connection. You'll need a *team* at some time, even if you haven't yet reached that point.

The Family and Medical Leave Act allows you to take an unpaid leave from your job to care for a family member in need. You must have worked at least 1,250 hours over the past twelve months to be eligible, and you may take up to twelve weeks a year. To find out more, visit dol.gov/dol/esa/whd/fmla.

Always have a Plan B.

Learn as you go; don't try to do everything all at once. Avoid information overload.

Take a seminar in caregiving. Such seminars are often offered through your local Red Cross or Area Agency on Aging (AAA). The National Association of Area Agencies on Aging can put you in touch with the

AAA in your neighborhood (see Resources). You can also find a free online class called "Caring for an Aging Parent" at thirdage.com.

## GETTING ORGANIZED

If you're generally a disorganized person, this is a good time to acquire new skills. Staying organized means keeping files for everything, including receipts, insurance company correspondence, and other useful items you'll want to have on hand for later reference.

Start with an accordion file. Dedicate yourself to maintaining it; it will make your life easier in so many ways.

Take inventory of the following documents and make a list of their locations. If most of the important documents are to be kept with your senior, consider making copies for you to keep at home. Some of these items may not apply to your senior, but keep track of those that do and take care of loose ends this list may remind you of:

- birth certificate
- social security card
- passport
- pension and retirement information
- Medicare card
- health insurance policies and card(s)
- prescription plan card
- medical assistance card
- disability insurance policy
- home insurance policy
- property deeds and titles
- rental or mortgage agreement
- will
- living will or advance directives
- health care directives

- medical proxy
- durable power of attorney
- checkbook
- deposit (bank) book
- safe deposit box key(s) and bank name
- investment records (stocks, bonds, etc.)
- car title(s) or registration(s)
- car insurance
- military records
- funeral instructions
- burial property information

Get a small notebook and use it as your caregiver diary. Keep lists of your parent's medications and their dosages. Make an entry for every health episode, describing the problem, the solution, the attending physician, and so forth. Keep this book with you always! This diary will serve as an invaluable document down the line when doctors require a complete history. (And it will save you from tearing your hair out when you are asked these questions umpteen times!)

If you are a high-tech type, a personal digital assistant (PDA) can become your best friend by organizing information on all of your senior's important documents and by holding multiple schedules (yours and your senior's) at the same time. There are even special programs designed specifically for keeping track of medications, medical records, and so forth.

Open a FedEx account. It will save your life at least once.

Supply Mom with a nice stack of stamped, return-addressed envelopes to make correspondence easier. You can even make up some labels with the addresses of people to whom she writes frequently.

▶ Get a big wall calendar. Make entries for everything and encourage your parent to consult it often.

▶ Help with letter writing when your parent can't seem to keep up with correspondence.

▶ Assist in making phone calls when letter writing is no longer possible.

▶ Whenever you decide to organize or rearrange things, let your father know about the changes, get his input if possible, and be patient as he readjusts. A frequent complaint of seniors with well-meaning loved ones who have reorganized things is that they can't find anything!

▶ Set up a fax machine in your parent's home. A fax machine can be useful if prescriptions are lost (and you have copies) or when important papers need to be consulted.

ᗒᖯ

---

"Mom hates anything electronic and would have held on to her rotary phone if the phone company hadn't objected. So getting her a fax machine seemed out of the question. But I had an extra one and set it up in her apartment, and you should have seen how pleased she was the first time a fax came through. It was my ten-year-old daughter's drawing of her with her grandma! She loved it, and even though she won't touch the machine (I change the paper and film when I go over there), she loves hearing it go off, because she knows she will have a special message from someone. Most important, she knows we are thinking of her throughout the day as we fax her scrawled messages, sometimes with just a big bunch of *X*s for the kisses we send her daily."

—*Lara Fein*

Establish routines. Seniors often lose track of time, especially after taking a nap.

Instituting routines will help structure the day.

Hang a large bulletin board and tack up everything from reminders and receipts to keys, eyeglasses, important phone numbers, orphaned earrings, and the like.

Keep an extra set of everything: keys, eyeglasses, hearing aids (keep the old one in case the new one gets lost), IDs, and so forth.

Keep photocopies of all your parent's important ID and membership cards. Highlight the expiration dates and leave a helpful reminder as to when the cards need to be renewed.

Keep an overnight bag in your car with a few of your own things (e.g., a toothbrush, a nightshirt, a change of clothes) just in case life throws you a curve. It will!

## FINANCIAL MATTERS

Cancel credit cards when they're rarely used, to simplify the mail—and your parent's life.

Phone and utility companies have special discounts and other services for seniors and the disabled: amplified phones, push-button phones, large-type bills, and so forth. Ask about what's available.

Keep track of your parents' finances, to the extent that they allow you to do so. Offer to help with bureaucratic problems and other details (like getting an insurance adjustment or renewing licenses) for which your parents might not have the patience.

▶ Respect that most people consider money to be a private subject, and handle it gently. Sometimes parents will open up about their finances, for example, if you mention your own concerns about retirement or estate planning. Ask their input on how they handled these matters.

▶ Recognize that giving up financial responsibilities represents a loss of control for many seniors. Don't take over all at once; perhaps Grandpa only needs help writing checks for now. Take it slowly.

▶ If you are in charge of your mother's finances, online banking will save you tons of time in bank visits and in being put on hold when you need to handle something. And you'll have an automatic record of every transaction.

▶ Arrange for your senior's social security, pension payments, and so forth, to be directly deposited into his bank account. It's a pretty simple process that the bank will be happy to help with, since it makes things easier on them, too.

▶ Check your senior's mail often to make sure outstanding debts are being paid, insurance premiums are up to date, and all business details are being handled.

〰️

"I knew it was really hard for my father to talk about financial issues, especially when it became clear that he might not be able to keep the house. We never really had a major 'talk' about it, where we sat down and ironed it all out. We did it in steps—I'd bring up one part of it, we'd talk a little, then I'd suggest that he take a week to think about it and we could continue the conversation after that. It took a while, but it really made a difference in how he dealt with it."

—*Chrissie Lawrence*

To be removed from mailing lists if those catalogs are getting to be too much, write to the Direct Marketing Association (DMA), Mail Preference Service, 1120 Avenue of the Americas, New York, NY 10036-6700 or visit the-dma.org.

Be sure to have copies of all health insurance and benefit program information that applies to your senior. Make a list of all this information and indicate which policies cover various needs. Does one policy, not another, cover dental care? Do any of them provide for home health care benefits? Should you consolidate policies? A geriatric caseworker can help you make these decisions.

One quick way to find benefit programs that your senior (or you) may be eligible for is to go online to benefitscheckup.org, sponsored by the National Council on the Aging. Fill out a confidential questionnaire, and get a list of local benefits or services that your senior (or you) may be qualified for.

Medical bills don't have to be paid for ninety days.

The IRS (Internal Revenue Service) and AARP have set up volunteer tax assistance programs for the elderly. (Accountants and tax lawyers volunteer their time to help with filling out tax returns.) Call 1-888-227-7669.

New caregiver tax benefits are in the works. Talk to an accountant to make sure you're getting the tax deductions, exemptions, and credits you might be eligible for as a caregiver. Or check with the IRS.

# Home Sweet Home

∾

## AROUND THE HOUSE

▶ Make your loved one's home pleasing to all of her senses. Potpourri, flowers, scented candles, music, cheerful decorations—even a soft teddy bear or stuffed animal, so soothing to us when we were children—all make a difference.

▶ Even if Mom can't manage a dog or cat, she may still enjoy having life in the house. Consider buying lower-maintenance pets such as birds (if she likes the sound of chirping!) or fish. Or bring friends' pets to visit. Perhaps she'd like to volunteer at the local animal shelter?

▶ Get a bird feeder and have it hung right outside a window that your parents gaze through often. Be sure to add bird food periodically. Buy them a field guide to birds, and ask them about the ones they've seen.

▶ It's never too late to learn to play a musical instrument.

You may have heard about research showing that nursing home residents who were given a plant to care for were happier and healthier than those who weren't. Aside from providing them with an activity and being pretty, plants release oxygen and can act as natural air purifiers. Just make sure none of them aggravate Dad's allergies.

Replace annual plantings in the garden with perennials. If your grandmother can no longer tend a beloved garden, would members of the local garden club volunteer to do the job?

Raised-bed gardening and smooth walkways make gardening possible for the wheelchair-bound. Be sure to get a tool bag that attaches to the chair.

Get wind chimes for the porch, the patio, or outside a window of your senior's favorite room—just not the bedroom.

Get book lights for various rooms.

Fill your senior's home with music. Inexpensive portable stereos can go in the bedroom, the kitchen, the porch, and the bathroom, assuming you take the necessary safety precautions.

You can help your loved one tell time with flowers.

ს‱

"By the age of seventy-seven, Aunt Renee could no longer keep track of time. Always the anxious type, she'd forget how much time there had been between visits, even though I went by twice a week like clockwork. Now I always make a point of picking up flowers for her when I go over, and I let her know that I will be back before they wilt."

—*Meg Shaefer*

No one says the living room has to be the living room and the bedroom has to be the bedroom. If stairs are a problem, or if it's just more convenient, turn the living room into the bedroom.

Make sure Mom has a nice easy chair or recliner available so she doesn't have to get into bed to relax. High-backed chairs offer better support than others. Learn about ergonomic furniture and other specially designed chairs that make standing up and sitting down much easier. You can find ergonomic furniture at most furniture stores.

Swivel seats at the dining table will be helpful for Dad if he has problems sitting down and standing up.

Just as timers (and alarm clocks) are useful in the kitchen, they can also be used as a medications reminder or as a way to time exercise routines. Get a few for other rooms of the house.

Covers that are 100 percent cotton are less likely to irritate or cause your loved one to perspire.

Install dimmer switches. Seniors are often light-sensitive, and dimmers afford flexibility.

Those rolling swivel tables that can slide over a bed or chair (called overbed tables) are starting to show up in designer furniture catalogs, probably because they make life easier for everyone. They're very handy in bedrooms and in living rooms.

Get one of those trays that can clip on to the arm of a sofa or armchair. It is a perfect holder for Mom's cup of tea, reading glasses, inhaler—the few little things she needs or wants right there close at hand.

Hang closet rods lower down to make them more accessible.

▶ Keep small occasional tables near chairs for frequently used items. If possible, get more than one of these items (e.g., glasses, pads of paper, pens), and keep them around the house in handy baskets on the tables to minimize the need for your senior to get up every time an item is needed.

▶ Poisons should be clearly labeled. Use brightly colored nail polish to make large *X*s across bottles and cans that should be avoided. Or better yet, keep them isolated *somewhere other than in the kitchen*.

▶ A footrest offers welcome relief for tired feet—and it makes a great gift.

▶ Minimize cluttering knickknacks that may become difficult for your father to clean. If they are of sentimental value, you can put them in a memory box and take them out when you visit.

▶ When you shop for furniture for your loved one, try to get him to accompany you or at least come to the store to try out something you've selected. If this is not possible, make sure the piece is returnable.

▶ Cable TV companies offer special services for seniors, such as enhanced audio and closed captioning. Check them out.

▶ If the door thresholds in your mother's home are higher than half an inch, install miniramps or transition wedges that will make getting across them easier, especially if she is in a wheelchair.

▶ U-shaped drawer pulls are easier to grip than knobs.

▶ Mirrors that tilt down, such as a chevalier mirror, accommodate people of all heights and needs.

So that Grandpa doesn't have to get up and search for the TV remote, attach strips of Velcro to the back of the remote and to the side of his favorite easy chair. Velcro dots can also be used to keep eyeglasses, pens, and even keys in place.

Lever-style handles are easier to operate than round doorknobs, which may be difficult to grip. Similarly, light switches with long levers are available from electrical supply houses and are easier to deal with than switches with short levers.

## HOME SAFE HOME

Learn the Heimlich maneuver and CPR at your local Red Cross or YMCA.

The Red Cross will send someone to your house to teach you any caregiving skills you may need. Many local chapters have additional services, such as Lifeline, available for seniors and their families. Call 1-877-272-7337.

A physical therapist can teach your senior to fall "correctly"—that is, with the least amount of injury. If mobility is an issue but physical therapy is not called for, you may still want to consult with a physical therapist for guidance.

Walk with your mother at *her* pace.

When assisting a senior who has difficulty walking, position yourself on his weaker side.

A cane should be the correct height for the user: the curve of the handle should be level with Dad's wrist if his arm is hanging at his side.

When installing any safety device or some other tool or item of furniture to make life easier for your parent, involve him in the decision to the extent that you're able. ("Would you like a walker with or without a basket?" "Which of these recliners works best for you?")

If a walker is needed, shop around. You can rent the generic type from the pharmacy until you locate the right one. Opt for the kind that has a basket in front. All walking aids should be measured and adjusted by a professional.

Check wheelchairs often for proper tire pressure and brake operation.

To maneuver a wheelchair up stairs, turn it around backward so the large wheels go up first. To go downstairs with a wheelchair, tilt the chair back and take each step slowly. Don't ever tip the wheelchair forward if someone is sitting in it.

Old-fashioned hot water bottles (yes, they still make them!) do the job and help avoid some of the safety problems that arise from electric pads and blankets. Or try one of the new packs you can heat in the microwave—just make sure it's not *too* hot!

If you need to make changes in your home when parents come to visit, have a list of "senior-proofing" measures on a bulletin board and assign these to various members of the family: Sarah clears away the knickknacks in the living room, Sam puts reflective tape on the edges of the stairs, Bonkers is moved to the basement (Mom's allergic to cats), and Jessie brings out Aunt Laura's ugly sculpture of the squirrel that Mom thinks is just the cutest thing in the whole world!

If you have questions about how safe your parent is at home, arrange to have a free geriatric care assessment. Someone will come to the home and review safety precautions and also your parent's ability to care for himself. Call the American Geriatric Society in New York (1-212-308-1414) to get a referral to the proper agency in your area.

If Grandma lives alone and you are concerned about her health or safety, have an agreed-upon time at which you call every day. Agree that she will let you know ahead of time if there will be a conflict that would keep her from answering.

If you're not able to check in with Dad yourself every day (or he gets annoyed if you do), there are different types of free community services designed for this purpose. They include telephone programs and services like Postal Alert, in which the mail carrier knocks on the door if the previous day's mail hasn't been collected—if there's no answer, the mail carrier calls a local service agency. Contact the local senior center and/or Red Cross and ask what specific services they offer in Dad's community.

Look into personal SOS devices, such as safety pendants with a button that Mom can press if she needs help. The market for these devices has exploded, and there is a huge variety available. One of the most popular companies selling these products is Lifeline. Call 1-800-LIFELINE (1-800-543-3546).

If you live in the same house with a disabled or memory-impaired parent (or when that parent visits), you can use a child monitor to keep track of your parent during the night and save yourself some worry. If you need to see what's happening, put an unobtrusive, portable "nanny cam" in the room.

Guard rails—the kind you see in showers—are also useful around the house, especially in hallways. Make sure all banisters on staircases are firmly affixed to the wall.

➤ Learn what you can about home health aids such as zipper pulls, grabbers, guard rails, and other safety and convenience devices. Talk to your pharmacist about the possibility of renting these items; be aware of the array of aids available. Check online or in the Yellow Pages for the largest medical supply houses to which you have access, and be sure to review their catalogs from time to time as the situation at home changes.

➤ Review safety precautions often, but don't lecture Dad or quiz him. Instead, *demonstrate*.

➤ Install tap lights or place flashlights in dark corners (closet shelves, on tables near stairs, etc.), but know that their batteries run out quickly if they're left on for any extended period.

➤ Keep a large flashlight or lantern in every closet that doesn't have a light.

➤ It's great to have fire extinguishers, but make sure you know how to use them, and teach your loved one.

➤ Nighttime can be disorienting for seniors. They may need guidance toward areas of the house that they would find easily by day.

❧

"We grew up in a small apartment in the Bronx, and when Mom first started staying with us, she was overwhelmed by the size of our four-bedroom, two-storied house. She'd get especially nervous at night about not being able to find her way to the bathroom and back. So we hung signs on the doors letting her know whose bedroom was whose, and we put little, round neon-colored stickers on the floor to guide her path to the bathroom. She was so grateful for the feeling of safety they gave her."

*—Bruce Ostreicher*

One of the most common accidents among seniors occurs when they bend over to pick up a dropped cane. Attach a wrist strap to a regular cane or get a cane with "legs."

Make sure that heavily trafficked routes remain uncluttered. Remove small chairs, tables, plants, and knickknacks that may interfere with your loved one's safety. Put them all in one area (a special shelf or an out-of-the-way tabletop) so they can still be enjoyed.

Smoking should not be tolerated. Smoking in bed should be completely outlawed. But if Dad is going to smoke anyway, set up a place where he can do it safely. Be realistic.

Install smoke alarms and check them often to make sure they're working properly. Familiarize your parent with the sound the alarm will make, in case there is a fire. Keep extra batteries around and make it a habit to change the batteries periodically; don't wait for the batteries to run low. It will be easy to remember these chores if you do them on holidays or specific dates, such as daylight saving time.

For the asking, the fire department will provide special stickers identifying windows of the disabled, so they can be located and rescued in case of emergency.

Install light-sensitive night-lights. Put regular lights on timers to be turned on at dusk.

Lower the water temperature to 120 degrees Farenheit to avoid any possibility of Mom getting seriously burned when she turns on the tap.

If your senior can't see the numbers on the clock, timer, oven, or stove, paint red dots with brightly colored nail polish to mark the appropriate places.

Install floodlights outside entrances to the house, and put them on a timer.

Movement-sensitive lights are useful if Dad keeps forgetting to turn on the basement light when he goes down there.

Check lightbulbs to make sure they all work. Replace them with long-life bulbs.

Use bicycle reflectors on stairs.

You should have a complete set of keys to your parents' dwelling (and try to find a trustworthy neighbor to keep a second set on hand). Keep their keys on your own key ring so you will have them with you at all times. Keep an extra key to their car.

People with mobility problems often have an easier time walking on surfaces that are not carpeted. (Carpeted stairs can be especially difficult to negotiate.) If this is the case and carpeting is a necessity, try industrial, low-pile styles. If you can't recarpet the area or if there's a particular trouble spot, you can buy an acrylic floor protector or an industrial-carpeted mat at an office supply store.

Make sure sidewalks are shoveled and leaves are removed at the appropriate times of year.

Make sure all doors and windows are easy to open and close from the inside.

Make a holder for the extra lengths of electrical cords that clutter the floor, by slicing a rubber ball open along one side. Push the sides open and stuff the cords inside.

## In the Kitchen

▶ Keeping spices in a drawer instead of on a shelf might make life easier for seniors who can't stretch easily. You can also keep often-used items in a basket left on a countertop.

▶ Make sure oven mitts are handy.

▶ If you've saved pennies and clipped coupons your whole life, this might be a good time to splurge—on paper plates. They're easier and more sanitary.

▶ Plastic or melamine plates are lighter and easier to handle than heavier ones.

▶ Lighting strips under kitchen cabinets will make work spaces easier to use.

▶ Consider replacing large appliances with smaller ones. Food processors now come in many sizes, and minichoppers and grinders are available in all styles. Toaster ovens and tabletop rotisseries are sometimes easier to deal with than a wall oven or one that requires lots of bending.

▶ If getting around the house is difficult for Mom, consider putting a minimicrowave or minifridge in the living room or bedroom.

▶ Lazy Susans in the refrigerator and in cabinets put all items within easy reach.

▶ Faucets with wide levers—as opposed to round knobs or other hard-to-handle devices—make life easier for seniors with joint problems.

The temperature in the refrigerator needs to be lower than 40 degrees Fahrenheit to preserve foods safely.

Any electrical outlet near any sink should have a grounded fault interrupter type socket assembly. Make sure there's one in the bathroom, too.

For some seniors, it's easier to cut foods like raw meat with shears instead of a knife. Keep a lightweight pair in the kitchen.

Encourage your senior to turn all pot handles in toward the center of the stove to avoid accidents.

When cooking for your own family, make extra portions and freeze them in individual serving containers for your loved one.

The microwave is safer than the conventional oven, and the convection oven cuts down on cooking time. Make sure your parent knows how to convert recipes.

Check the food supply often to make sure your parent is shopping for nutritious, well-rounded meals and that foods past the expiration date are discarded. Make sure that spoiled foods are removed promptly and that all foods are stored properly.

Get your parent a convenient jar opener. A rubber glove is great for this purpose.

Encourage your loved one to use smaller, lightweight pots and pans, which are easier to handle.

Familiarize yourself with kitchen aids that can make a senior's life easier. You can use the kitchen section of seniorshops.com as a starting point.

Keep a stool in the kitchen so Mom can sit when she works at the counter.

Buy a bagel cutter that holds a bagel in place, making it easier to slice.

An electric potato peeler ensures a steady supply of those potato pancakes Dad can't live without.

Hang a Peg-Board in the kitchen and keep often-used items hanging from "S" hooks so your loved one doesn't have to bend and stretch as often.

Loop a dish towel through the refrigerator handle. It's easier for arthritic hands to pull the door open this way.

Place a block of wood in the back of the refrigerator to use as a shelf so items in the back will be higher up and easier to locate.

Plastic frames with handles for holding milk and juice containers make lifting them easier.

Take off cabinet doors or install open shelves to make supplies more accessible.

You can get an oven with a door that opens from side to side, which is easier for a person in a wheelchair. Also side-by-side refrigerator-freezers and dishwashers installed eight inches higher than usual help make the kitchen a place where *all* family members are welcome.

If Mom loves making stews and soups and has to lug heavy pots filled with water across the kitchen from the sink to the stove, get a hose attachment that will allow her to fill the pot after she places it on the stove.

A long-handled grabber will allow Dad to get at items that are high up in the pantry without straining. They're actually great all over the house, but having one especially for the kitchen ensures that it'll be there when he needs it.

All appliances should have automatic shutoff features.

All appliances should have easy-to-read dials. If they're difficult to read, get replacements for them or mark the important positions such as "Off" and "On" clearly with red nail polish.

## In the Bathroom

There are hundreds of bathroom fixtures and gadgets that will make life for a senior easier and a lot safer. Obtain a catalog from one of the many mail-order companies that will ship these supplies, and review their offerings each time your loved one's situation changes. Items you may never have considered at one moment may become lifesavers the next.

Without being *too* intrusive, try to keep track of how well your senior is doing with bathroom skills. (That's where most accidents happen.)

Try to minimize clutter in the bathroom, and keep all plug-in appliances well away from the sink, toilet, and bathtub.

Install guard rails not only in the bath but also alongside the toilet and anywhere else they might be useful.

Seniors often seem to have a fear of showering or bathing. But often, the *real* fear is the fear of falling. Reassure them and install safety grips that will give them confidence.

Long-handled brushes and sponges make bathing easier.

Handheld showerheads are indispensable for seniors. Install a long-corded handheld showerhead in the shower for washing hair or taking a seated shower. Or just buy a shower hose to connect to the faucet as a less expensive option.

If there's an intercom in the house, install a unit in the bathroom. A senior who has fallen and can't get up should have some way to get help.

Install liquid soap and shampoo dispensers in the shower to avoid clutter and the whole dropped-the-soap-went-to-pick-it-up-then-slipped-and-fell routine.

A shower seat will allow your senior to sit in a comfortable position while bathing. But don't use just any plastic stool, even if it has rubber feet. Buy one that's made just for this purpose.

Replace faucets with lever handles, which can be pushed into position rather than turned.

Wall-to-wall industrial carpeting in the bath—as opposed to rugs—will minimize accidents.

An elevated toilet seat, which is about three to four inches higher than a regular toilet seat, is easier for seniors to negotiate, since it causes less strain on the back and legs.

If Mom needs your help with bathing and other personal functions, a little music can make the experience more sociable and less awkward. Try a small portable stereo or a shower radio. Conversation is nice, too. Or hum.

Urge your loved one to gather everything she'll need in the shower or tub before she gets in. If you assist with bathing, have everything ready—and the tub filled—before you bring Mom in for her bath.

▶ Learn how to wash hair. If Dad is bedridden, have him lie on his back with his head over the foot of the bed, with supporting pillows under his neck and shoulders and a bowl beneath his head. You can buy an inflatable hair-washing tray that will minimize the mess.

▶ When washing your mother's hair, apply petroleum jelly around her face along her hairline to keep water from dripping into her eyes.

▶ If your senior is very modest and you must bathe him, do not undress him fully. Bathe just one part of the body at a time.

▶ When giving a sponge bath, be sure to use a different sponge for the genital area than you use for the rest of the body. As you wash your mother, cover the area that is not being washed to keep her warm. Make sure you dry her thoroughly when you're done.

▶ If it's a same-sex parent, you can save some time and hassle and shower together.

▶ To be really safe, remove all electrical appliances from the bathroom.

▶ If there's a lock on the bathroom door, remove it.

▶ Newspapers are better than towels for mopping up water, and you can just throw them away when you're done.

## CRIME PROTECTION

▶ Self-defense classes especially for seniors can empower your loved one as well as provide a great social atmosphere and—who knows?— maybe even save a life. Ask your local agency on aging what's available in the neighborhood. Or consider arranging private lessons through a local martial arts center.

Especially if other caregivers are present, keep valuables locked away.

If you need to hide valuables for any reason, make sure your parent knows where you have put everything. A faulty memory may cause her to think her precious things have been stolen. Perhaps this might be a good time to distribute some of these things among the family—with her permission, of course.

Complicated alarm systems can become more trouble than they're worth and often end up not getting used. Install a burglar alarm, but make sure it is simple enough to be usable.

Periodically demonstrate to your senior how to operate the burglar alarm.

Sad as it may be, as much as 50 percent of all telephone scams and similar fraud is perpetrated on the elderly. Among other reasons, seniors are considered good targets because they are more easily reachable at home, they tend to have available funds, and they are more reluctant to be "impolite" to salespeople.

Let your loved one know that she is at risk for fraud. Some of the more common scams aimed at seniors include the following:

- claiming that the senior has won a free gift or a sweepstakes prize, but the caller needs a credit card, social security number, and/or bank information for verification purposes
- offering "free" medical equipment, with a "guarantee" that the senior's insurance will reimburse for it
- "slamming"—when a phone company switches your service to another provider without your permission
- offering to do free radon or other similar testing in the home
- asking that the senior call a telephone number with a long-distance area code—often 809, a Caribbean area code—that can cost as much as $25 a minute

Many police departments sponsor special crime prevention education programs for older folks, often in conjunction with a local senior center. They can educate your senior about making the home safer, avoiding scams, and so forth.

Make sure peepholes are accessible (sometimes seniors shrink!) and that they are used appropriately. If a family member is wheelchair-bound, have a second peephole installed at his level.

A doorbell that doubles as an intercom provides extra security.

While mail, phone, and Internet scams are more common, some con artists show up at the front door. In these scenarios, someone may come to "inspect" the house, a contractor "notices" that the house needs work and can do it cheaply, or a technician shows up to provide "free" rug shampooing or other cleaning services. Discuss these situations periodically to establish safe ground rules.

## How to Protect Your Senior Against Fraud

The National Consumers League's National Fraud Information Center (NFIC) at 1-800-876-7060 or fraud.org has a special division devoted to protecting seniors. The NFIC can counsel you and your senior about whether a particular suspicious situation is most likely a fraud and help you deal with it. The NFIC can also warn you about new scams to be aware of and can help victims of fraud by providing support and reassurance, as well as getting them in touch with the proper law enforcement agencies.

Make sure you and your senior understand the following:
- Legitimate salespeople are willing to provide contact information for their organization and are willing to send written informa-

tion about the products or services they're selling. If a salesperson is not willing to do these things, something is fishy.

■ Legitimate salespeople don't ask for bank account or social security information. The only times seniors should need to provide their social security number are when dealing with a financial institution from which they are requesting a loan or credit card account.

■ Legitimate companies don't pressure people into sending money immediately. They don't ask that funds be wired or that the customer send cash via messenger.

■ It's illegal for contests or sweepstakes to require payment to enter or claim a prize.

■ Legitimate companies never ask for credit card information for identification purposes. The only time credit card numbers should be given is when buying actual products or services.

■ Law enforcement agencies never ask for payment from people they are trying to help. They don't ask for financial information or credit card numbers either (except possibly if *you* contact *them* about fraud).

■ All legitimate charities are happy to provide potential donors with their organization's financial information, tax-exempt ID number, and a means for verifying their nonprofit status.

Today's seniors come from a generation in which (for better and worse) politeness was more highly valued than it is today. Many of them are very reluctant to be rude by hanging up on callers, even when they are being hounded. This is one of the reasons they are so heavily targeted by scam artists. Communicate to your senior in a positive, supportive way that it is OK to hang up on telemarketers (or slam the door on pushy "visitors").

If you request that callers remove your name and number from their telemarketing lists, they are required by law to do it. Encourage your senior to do this. If the same company calls again, tell the caller that you will report him to the Better Business Bureau.

If your father receives a suspicious call, he should say that he wants to check with the Better Business Bureau about the caller's organization and ask for a number to call back. If the caller refuses to give the number or insists on an immediate decision, the organization is not legitimate.

It is harder to get scammed if you don't pick up the phone! Get caller ID (it is available with a large display for easier viewing) and an answering machine. Suggest that your parent does not answer the phone if she doesn't recognize the caller's name. Others can leave messages.

To get a name removed from telemarketing lists, write to the Direct Marketing Association (DMA), Telephone Preference Service, 1120 Avenue of the Americas, New York, NY 10036-6700 or visit the-dma.org. Your state may also manage a "do not call list" for which you can register.

Warning signs that your senior is already being targeted include the following:

- She receives frequent (often repeated) calls regarding sweepstakes, investment opportunities, or requests for donations from charities.
- He gets tons of junk mail for contests, "free" trips, prizes, and sweepstakes.
- She gets lots of cheap merchandise (such as costume jewelry, mugs, pens and pencils, beauty products, etc.) in the mail as "prizes" that required expensive shipping and handling costs.
- He is asked to wire payments or send them via courier services.

- She makes repeated and/or large payments to out-of-state companies, and strange listings appear on her credit card statements.
- He gets calls from organizations offering to recover money that he has paid to telemarketers, for a fee.

If you notice any of these warning signs, contact the National Fraud Information Center at 1-800-876-7060 for immediate help. In addition, you can write to the Federal Communications Commission, Consumer Protection Branch, Mail Stop 1600A2, Washington, DC 20554. You can also file a complaint for all types of fraud with your local attorney general's office and local Better Business Bureau.

Once your loved one is identified as a target (and especially if he's actually paid up on a scam), the word often gets out and calls start pouring in. If the situation is very bad, change his phone number and get a new, unlisted one.

Be patient and understanding with your senior about marketing scams. Don't make her feel ashamed. *Many* intelligent people have fallen for these tricks.

# Keeping It Together

❧

## Dress for Success

There's no need to throw all fashion sense out the window just because your senior's needs or abilities are changing. There are mail-order clothing companies dedicated to making fairly stylish clothes for people with special needs like arthritis, limited mobility, or incontinence. One such company is Silvert's, at 1-800-387-7088 (call for a catalog) or silverts.com; another is Caring Concepts, at 1-800-336-2660 or caringconcepts.com.

Keep clothes simple and easy to care for. Buy wardrobes in mix-and-match colors. Get machine-washable clothes for the most part. But don't do away altogether with certain luxury items (e.g., silk scarves or a special outfit or two).

Getting dressed once can be difficult enough. Help your loved one avoid having to take clothes off and put them right back on again the other way around, by labeling the inside of pants and sweaters "front" and "back."

Make clothing easier to manage by replacing buttons with snaps and finding shoes with Velcro closures.

Replace small buttons with larger ones, or buy a set of button covers that simply slip over existing buttons.

A drop of superglue applied to the center of a button once it's been sewn on will keep the button in place forever.

Shop for bras with front closures.

Take a lesson from your ski parka. If you thread a small length of ribbon through the hole in a zipper pull and tie it, it's much easier to grab. Bright colors are great if Dad has trouble seeing the zipper in the first place, but basic black is more discreet for pants and other more formal attire.

Make dressing easier by putting the shirt inside the sweater so your senior can put both on at once. He can put on underpants and trousers the same way.

Too many wardrobe choices can be overwhelming.

ᘒᗡ

"Mom hated shopping, but she loves looking good and keeping up with current styles. Now I go to the store for her and pick out some different things I think she'll like. We have a wonderful fashion show—Dad is our audience—and I return the rejects before they show up on my credit card. If Mom is tired one day, we just try on a few things and save the rest for the next day. Dad loves this routine: now he doesn't have to spend hours sitting in the 'husband's chair' at the store while he helps Mom shop."

—*Maureen McLaughlin*

▶ Help organize your senior's closet—you can even assemble outfits and leave them handy for dressing. Just make sure he knows where everything is, and let him participate in deciding how it will all be organized.

▶ If Mom has a walk-in closet loaded with a lifetime of fashions, you might want to section off a small part of it in which you keep everything she uses on a day-to-day basis. It's easier to keep a smaller section within the larger closet clean and organized. It'll be easier for you to take inventory—and easier for her to find things.

▶ Be sensitive to room temperatures, and make sure Grandpa's dressed appropriately.

▶ Getting a coat on someone in a wheelchair can be difficult. Capes are better, but make sure the hem is well clear of the wheels and spokes; in fact, there are special capes designed just for wheelchair users.

▶ It's important that your loved ones get dressed every day, even if there's no compelling reason to do so. Getting dressed signals the start of a new day and can keep spirits up when the situation warrants otherwise. Communicate this to caregivers, and encourage your parents to dress daily. Tell Dad how nice he looks in that shirt or how just a bit of lipstick really perks up Mom's look. And don't stop buying them new things just because they seem to have enough to wear. A new blouse for her or a sweater for him are reminders that there's a future ahead.

▶ Even if you don't make purchases through catalogs, they're useful for viewing styles, considering choices, and agreeing on colors. This saves time and confusion when you're shopping together or will allow you to do a better job of shopping for your senior on your own.

Pants and skirts with elastic waistbands are easiest to slip on and off. You can convert a pair of your father's favorite regular-waisted pants by sewing a short length of elastic into the sides and back where they won't show.

Elastic shoelaces allow your senior to slip shoes off without untying them.

If Grandma can't seem to part with some of the clothing she no longer needs—and closet space is at a premium—assure her that you will have the pieces donated to a charity she cares about and that they'll be cherished by their new owners.

If you're laying out clothing for your parent, lay them out in the order in which they will be put on—underwear on top, then the shirt, then the pants, and so forth. Tuck a sock into each shoe.

As an alternative to wool, synthetic fleece clothing is breathable, is relatively nonstainable, doesn't scratch, and can adjust to changes in temperature. It's especially great for seniors with circulation problems who are sensitive to drafts and cold temperatures.

Give Dad a reason to look forward to getting dressed each day.

∽

"It has become the best part of the day. I put off dressing him until after the kids are off to school so I can spend the time I need. While I dress him, I tell him stories and we joke around. When I reach around his back to get his sweater on, there's always a kiss on his cheek, because, I tell him, 'I was in the neighborhood anyway.' Our little games are silly, but they're fun, and starting out the day with love can only be a good thing."

—*Shirley Netherland*

Keep types of clothing together in the closet—pants in one section, then shirts, dresses, and so on.

Buy multiple sets of pajamas, so if half gets ruined your father will still have a set.

Make sure your senior's shoes have rubber soles and that they are maintained. If dress shoes are to be worn, sandpaper the bottoms if they're slippery.

People sometimes shrink as they get older, so your loved one may need smaller clothes. Try shopping in petite sizes for women, or check out youth clothing for men.

While we mostly get smaller with age, our feet expand; make sure your loved one has correctly sized shoes.

Hats are great for bad hair days, they provide protection from the sun, and they're fun to collect.

Loved ones with sensitive skin will find cotton to be less irritating than wool or synthetics.

Buy all or most of Dad's socks in the same style so he won't have to worry about strays.

Mom will never lose her hearing aid again if you ask the audiologist to attach an alligator clip, which allows her to clip the hearing aid to her collar.

Check your loved one's pockets regularly for holes and for lost items.

Get slip-on shoes. If closures are absolutely necessary for support, go for Velcro.

Preknotted ties can make life a little easier for your father if he suffers from arthritis.

If your parents like to take walks at night, encourage them to wear reflective clothing.

If Mom insists on wearing the same thing day after day, buy multiples of that outfit.

Buying shoes can be difficult for seniors who have little patience or energy for shopping. If you find a style that works, buy an extra pair.

Long-handled shoehorns, which are readily available, will make it easier for Dad to put on his shoes without having to reach all the way to his feet.

A dressing stick, available where other health aids are sold, makes dressing a lot easier and will keep your parent independent for longer.

## LOOKING GOOD, FEELING GOOD

Help seniors maintain personal habits. If Mom routinely had a manicure once a week, make sure she keeps getting them. If necessary, find beauticians and manicurists who will make house calls.

Give Grandma a manicure yourself! Manicures can be a soothing, intimate experience. Even just a good hand massage with plenty of lotion can be renewing and invigorating. If your loved one fidgets, give her a manicure when she's sleepy.

Pedicures are excellent for increasing circulation in the feet and legs.

Don't avoid jewelry just because it's inconvenient to put on. Get Mom some necklaces that go over the head, watches and bracelets that slip on and don't pinch, and small earrings she can wear comfortably.

Is your senior's old jewelry still comfortable now that sizing may have changed? Get rings and wristbands adjusted when needed. If a favorite ring no longer fits, put it on a chain to be worn as a necklace.

Help Mom simplify her makeup routine—a little eye shadow, some blush, and lip gloss applied delicately can go a long way.

Ask your pharmacist for a good dry shampoo, which your senior can use when a real shampoo isn't practical. This comes in the form of a powder that you apply and then brush out. It won't take the place of a nice soapy shampoo, but it'll do in a pinch.

Get your father an electric razor for shaving—it's much safer and easier to use than blades.

A pretty scarf can brighten up an outfit, and it can double as a bib if Mom's too modest to use one. Just have others handy to replace any that might get soiled.

You may appreciate a good magnifying mirror for plucking eyebrows or clipping nose hairs, but it can be a godsend to your loved one while applying makeup, shaving, or combing and styling hair. Find one of the larger wall-mounting ones to put in the bathroom. A handheld magnifying mirror makes a nice gift.

A rubber band around a lipstick tube or other cylindrical object will make it easier to grip.

Many salons offer free haircuts given by their trainees. Call and ask if your senior can participate.

The large cosmetics counters at most department stores offer tons of free samples just for the asking. Don't forget to ask!

If Mom has worn pierced earrings her whole life and is just now beginning to have problems—a stinging sensation or earrings turning black—she may have developed a skin allergy to the metal that the earrings are made of. Have her try a pair with surgical steel posts that have the look of silver.

Put your mother's glasses on an eyeglass chain, which she can wear around her neck when she's not wearing her glasses. The ones made out of fabric-colored foam rope are light and comfy.

Let your loved one know that her options are open.

∽

"After chemo, Mom lost some of her hair. You couldn't really tell, since she'd had thick hair to begin with. But Mom fussed about it until we suggested a wig. Ultimately, she agreed that she didn't need one, but I think it made her happy to know that we would take whatever measures were necessary to make her comfortable. It really improved her outlook!"

—Jan Rodriguez

# 4

# Managing the Outside World

෬

## GETTING OUT AND ABOUT

Know the route that Grandpa takes to his regular daytime activities.

Make sure Mom carries identification and *your* contact information with her whenever she's out of the house.

Check that your senior's car is well maintained. Check often for problems with windshield wipers, tires, and brakes.

Even those who drive safely by day may suffer night blindness, which is common among seniors. Ride along with your loved one periodically at different times of day to assess these skills.

AARP (formerly the American Association of Retired Persons) offers a course called 55/ALIVE for mature drivers. It's designed to help troubleshoot a lot of the problems seniors develop in driving. If you suspect your loved one needs help, insist he take this course. It may help convince him if you let him know he'll probably get a reduction in his car insurance when he completes the course. Call toll-free at 1-888-227-7669 or go to aarp.org/55alive.

A problem seniors often have with night driving is that they're more likely to be "blinded" by bright headlights. There are special glare-reduction glasses your senior can wear to avoid this problem.

Remove the distributor cap from Mom's car or take the keys if she shouldn't be driving but is being really stubborn about it. Loss of the ability to drive can be extremely upsetting for seniors—many consider it to be the single most difficult change they face. Recognize this and work to set up practical transportation alternatives so Mom won't feel completely stranded.

Take the time to teach Dad necessary public transportation routes (to and from the senior center, etc.). Accompany him the first few times to make sure he knows what to do in case there are glitches.

Great gift idea: a small change purse filled with a supply of transportation tokens or the correct change if your mother's using a senior discount pass.

Locate special senior transportation services through the Yellow Pages, the local Area Agency on Aging, and senior centers. Some services will bring seniors anywhere they need to go, while others may be limited to health care appointments, food shopping, and so forth.

Many individual organizations provide transportation to and from their facilities or meetings. Examples are hospital or senior center shuttles, or church or synagogue carpools. Make sure to look into these options if Mom needs a way to get to the doctor's office or to Sunday services.

If you add up the expense of owning a car—paying for insurance, gas, and maintenance, plus tolls—it might not come out to much more than your parent would spend if he hired a private car service, assuming he doesn't drive more than a few times a week. What a luxury!

Arrange for a responsible teenage personal escort to help your parent on shopping trips and other excursions.

Almost all local stores offer home delivery: groceries, pharmacies, laundries, and the like. Use these services as freely as possible. Keep their phone numbers with you at all times.

Get to know the people who see your senior every day: the neighbors, store owners, and mail carriers. They can be a valuable source of information when you need it.

When waiters are especially kind and patient with your party, be sure your gratitude is reflected in your tip. Let everyone around you know that helping seniors is good for us all.

ഗ

"My daughter got her driver's license a few months ago, and of course she is always lobbying to borrow my car. We have a deal: if she takes her grandmother on an outing once a week (to the library or one of the other places Mom likes), then she gets the car for Saturday night. She's a pretty responsible driver anyway, but having my mother in the car reminds her to be extra careful. And while the museum with Grandma isn't as exciting as the movies with her friends, I think she and my mother both enjoy it."

—*Rodney Banks*

If Mom needs a walker but is too modest to make the change, she might just take a nice sturdy shopping cart with her when she goes out. *It won't take the place of a walker*, since it's not made for that purpose, but maybe she'll come to see that she really does need the extra support and relent.

∽

---

### Twenty Good Outings

1. Visit the library.
2. Wander through a museum (one that has rooms with places to sit).
3. Take in a movie.
4. Go to the theater.
5. Visit an aquarium.
6. Volunteer together at a library or anywhere in the community.
7. Get a manicure together.
8. Visit a florist or nursery just to smell the roses.
9. Take a walk in the park.
10. Attend a lecture.
11. Visit a friend at a nursing home.
12. Go to the opera.
13. Attend religious services.
14. Walk a dog from the local humane society.
15. Visit a cemetery.
16. Go to a child's recital, even if you don't know the child all that well.
17. Browse through a flea market.
18. Go to a pet store to watch the puppies and kittens.
19. Shop at the mall (one that offers free wheelchairs).
20. Hang out at a neighborhood coffee shop where you're likely to meet up with other seniors.

▶ Try to take excursions during slow or off-peak hours if your loved one tends to get overwhelmed.

▶ Many theater, opera, music, and other arts organizations have special senior discount programs. For example, the Theatre Development Fund in New York City (tdf.org) provides special offers to seniors and people with disabilities for Broadway and off-Broadway shows.

▶ Most malls, museums, and large parks make wheelchairs available to those who need them.

▶ A doorway must be at least thirty-two inches wide in order for a wheelchair to fit through; check before you travel or visit if you suspect there might be a problem.

▶ Get a portable folding seat to take on outings.

▶ Search out movie theaters with easy access. Report those that are not disability or senior friendly to the local Area Agency on Aging.

▶ Everybody has their typical high and low periods during the day. Schedule outings for the time of day when your loved one tends to have the most energy.

◈

"It takes a while for Dad to get going in the morning, and he sometimes gets nervous and agitated later in the day, but he's most like himself in the late morning and midday. So once a week we go out for a little shopping and a nice lunch."

—*Doug Benard*

▶ Seek out accommodating restaurants that offer senior discounts. If your favorite eatery doesn't offer any, ask the manager about it and let her know that perhaps she's not aware of how many seniors she'd attract if she offered the same discounts as the competition. Do this privately. Never embarrass your parent by causing a scene on his behalf.

▶ Bring snacks on outings. One with a good mix of carbohydrates and protein will keep everyone's energy and spirits up. Some suggestions:
- crackers and peanut butter
- string cheese and an apple or orange
- energy bars like Balance and ZonePerfect
- trail mix

▶ If your mother has a dog that she takes on walks, make sure the pet has your contact information on his tags, just to be extra safe. Attach the tags to a reflective collar and leash to make the perfect "gift set" for Fido.

▶ Waiters and waitresses can better help your party if they know what your special needs might be. Call ahead.

༄

"We love taking Dad out to eat—he's a gourmet from way back and thankfully has no dietary restrictions—but it requires patience. And since I hate to embarrass him by explaining his situation out loud, I have printed up little cards that I hand to the person who seats us. It says, 'Please be patient with our party. My dad has memory problems and will need extra help with his order. Also, please remove the knife from his place setting and have his food cut up in the kitchen. We're grateful to you for your help.' This makes life easier for everyone, Dad maintains his dignity in public, and of course, we tip appropriately."

—Lorraine Ferber

# TRAVEL

▶Statistics tell us that active seniors are healthier seniors. Since they get so much out of the experience, it's a good idea to encourage vacations and trips when possible. Research the many books, organizations, and websites geared toward senior travel.

▶Elderhostel (1-877-426-8056 or elderhostel.org) organizes terrific moderately priced adventure and learning programs—including astronomy, zoology, and just about everything in between—for people over the age of fifty-five.

▶Senior Globe (seniorglobe.com) offers information about current travel discounts available to seniors.

▶Visit about.com and type in the phrase "senior travel resources" to connect with senior travel groups and learn about special discounts.

▶For information about senior and special-needs travel (including transportation, lodging, discounts, and wheelchair and scooter rental, among other things), visit access-able.com. The Society for Accessible Travel and Hospitality (sath.org or 1-212-447-7284) also has information for travelers with disabilities and special needs.

▶The International Association for Medical Assistance to Travellers (1-716-754-4883 or iamat.org) can connect you with English-speaking doctors in almost any foreign country, in addition to providing a bunch of other services after you join (for free).

▶Most airlines offer a 10 percent discount to travelers sixty-two years and older, and some even offer coupon booklets that allow seniors to purchase round-trip tickets for travel anywhere in the United States for $300. Of course, restrictions apply. Call the individual airlines for more information.

Traveling by train is a great alternative for seniors for whom flying is not viable. Amtrak offers a variety of special discounts for seniors, including 15 percent off regular fares and special group rates. Call 1-800-USA-RAIL (1-800-872-7245) or visit amtrak.com.

How about a free vacation? Various government agencies as well as individual state park systems welcome senior volunteers to work as campground hosts in exchange for free lodging. Your parents could volunteer for a day or a year. Contact National Park Service, Volunteers-in-Parks Coordinator, 1849 C Street NW, Suite 7312, Washington, DC 20240, nps.gov/volunteer.

You'll be thrilled to know that once your parents reach the age of seventy-five, their ski lift tickets are usually free!

Keep a travel bag in the car with the supplies and provisions you need often: a small bottle of water, wet wipes, an extra pair of sunglasses, a barf bag like the kind you see on airplanes, and so forth.

Make your own wet wipes by placing napkins in a plastic container and adding baby oil. Turn the container upside down and right side up occasionally to allow the oil to penetrate.

Those little handheld fans can be a lifesaver if Mom has to wait in line for any period in a stuffy room or if it's hot out. Try to buy the kind that has a spray attachment for water so she gets a cool mist as well as a breeze.

Before you and your parents travel to a foreign country, make sure you know about illnesses you might encounter in the country you're visiting. Contact any of the following: World Health Organization (1-202-974-3000), Centers for Disease Control and Prevention (1-404-332-4559), and International Association for Medical Assistance to Travellers (1-716-754-4883).

▶Because seniors are more susceptible to childhood and local diseases as well as the flu and pneumonia, it's important to consult a doctor about immunizations before setting off on vacations. In addition to getting your senior those immunizations required by immigration laws, you should ask about other illnesses common to older travelers.

▶Before you take a trip, call your loved one's medical insurer to make sure that coverage will remain in place while you are traveling.

▶If Dad has special needs where lodging is concerned (e.g., wheelchair accessibility, specific types of linens), call ahead to make sure the room and grounds will accommodate his needs.

▶When traveling, always keep a list of important medical information with you: medications and their dosages, your loved one's physician's name and phone number, insurance information, and someone to contact in case of emergency. Personal identification should be carried at all times. Even if you're traveling without your loved one, keep important information (his doctors' phone numbers, a list of his medications) handy in case long-distance caregiving becomes necessary.

▶Travel insurance ensures that you get a refund or rebooking if a medical or family crisis prevents traveling. Most—but not all—airlines will honor these situations whether or not you have travel insurance. Ask about their policies when you purchase your tickets.

▶Someone at home should have your travel itinerary so you can be contacted if necessary.

▶Order special meals on flights forty-eight hours in advance to make sure you're accommodated. Confirm your orders at the time you check in. Or consider bringing your own "picnic."

Most airlines provide companions not only for children flying alone but for the elderly as well.

When booking flights, ask for a bulkhead seat—it's roomier.

If oxygen will be needed for a traveler with a cardiac condition, it should be ordered forty-eight hours before the flight.

When flying, make sure all important items, like medications, extra glasses, and so forth, are carried on along with a change of clothes.

If you're checking luggage that contains medication (which you should try not to do), keep at least two days' worth with you at all times. Pack a few extra days' meds in case your return home is delayed. Keep copies of prescriptions with you.

Make sure you and your loved one both drink plenty of fluids (eight ounces per hour), and get up and stretch and (if at all possible) take a walk down the aisle of the cabin periodically.

Many medications are affected by climate and environmental changes, sun exposure, heat, and cold. Ask the doctor about these, and also inquire about the possible side effects of drugs taken right before plane flights. Amnesia-like states and motion sickness are common side effects for some medications. It may be wise to withhold certain meds until after you've arrived at your destination. (Surprisingly, seniors are less susceptible to jet lag than the rest of us.)

Hotels offer sitter services. Make use of them in the day as well as the evening. Some seniors are slow to rise in the morning. A companion for a few hours in the morning will ensure that Dad will have energy left for the special dinner you've planned.

If it's difficult for Grandma to climb into your SUV, keep a small collapsible stool in your car that she can use to get in and out of the car.

Encourage your loved one to take bottled water on all outings, especially if he'll need to take medication.

Seniors needn't interrupt exercise routines just because they are traveling. Especially since traveling can be exhausting, it's important to stay in shape by maintaining a regular routine or at least a modified version of it. Exercise will also reduce the chance of injury. Make use of hotel and local gyms. Bring lightweight exercise gadgets with you and encourage stretching. Of course, there's always walking.

Buy a prepaid phone card for Mom, and make sure she knows how to use it, in case she needs to use a pay phone in an emergency.

# PART II

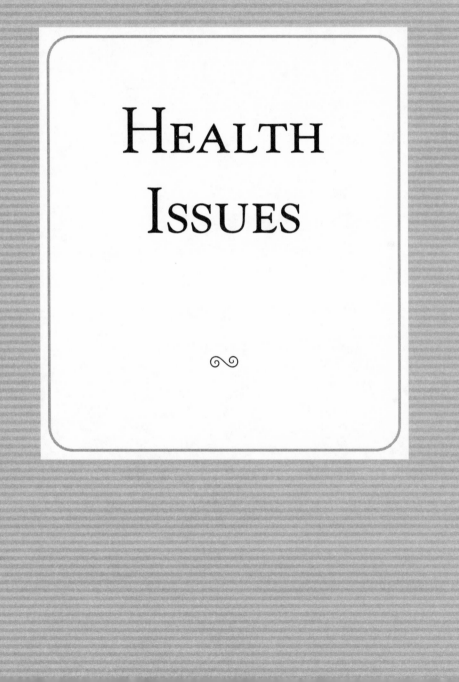

# HEALTH
# ISSUES

# 5

# Staying Healthy

∽

## SOUND BODY, SOUND MIND

*Everyone* needs a checkup regularly. But some seniors (and juniors!) reason that since they just saw the doctor last month about that sinus problem, they don't need to go again. A visit to the doctor for a specific problem doesn't take the place of a complete checkup.

Make sure your father is getting a balanced diet. Accompany him to the market to guide shopping choices, teach him to read labels, and discuss the importance of all the food groups, vitamins, fiber, and calcium.

ID jewelry with pertinent medical alert and contact information should be worn by all seniors. There is a huge variety of bracelets, pendants, and even watchbands available, many of them quite attractive, in stainless steel, sterling silver, and gold. Two companies that sell them are American Medical Identifications (1-800-363-5985 or americanmedical-id.com) and Medic Care Inc. (1-561-748-0840 or mediccareinc.com).

▶ Know your mother's baseline—what's "normal" for her. Some seniors have a lower normal body temperature than 98.6 degrees Farenheit, and others have had chronic problems throughout their lives. Be familiar with Mom's "default setting," and be aware of changes. Know that baselines change as a person ages. If, for instance, she goes through surgery, chances are she will come out of it with a new baseline.

▶ Know your loved one's complete medical history and keep a record of it to be taken to doctor's appointments and checked often. Just as important is to know your own medical history, in case genetic issues arise or transplants or transfusions become necessary.

▶ Water, water, water (for senior and caregiver). Unless it is contraindicated by a doctor, you should each be drinking eight glasses of water a day. Did you know that dehydration is a common cause of many disorders in the elderly, including urinary tract infections and circulation problems?

▶ Make sure liquids are available all day long. How about an attractive thermos for the bedside or a water cooler in the living room and on the patio? Get one on casters so it can be moved from room to room.

▶ Blood pressure is an issue among most elderly. Get a reliable sphygmomanometer (a blood pressure monitor) and teach your loved one—and yourself—to take blood pressure readings. Some pharmacies take blood pressure readings and teach you to do it yourself for free.

▶ At any given time, the National Institutes of Health Clinical Center has almost 1,000 programs under way that study and test the newest medical procedures, including cancer, heart disease, and Alzheimer's treatments. If your mother qualifies, she may get free health care at their 540-bed hospital in Bethesda, Maryland. Call their toll-free hotline: 1-800-411-1222.

▶ Local community service organizations such as the Kiwanis or Lions Club often offer free eye exams and eyeglasses to seniors who can't easily afford them. Your Area Agency on Aging will tell you what's available in your area.

▶ Free dental care is available from local dental schools, and often, a low income is not even a requirement. Contact the dental college in your area.

▶ Keep a diary of your senior's health progress.

▶ If your loved one is running a temperature or experiencing any other condition that may require a doctor's care, keep hourly notes and temperature readings for later reference.

▶ Wash your hands often when caring for your parents. Wash theirs as well.

▶ Keep plenty of moisturizer around for your hands and Dad's. Dry, chapped hands are especially common in winter. When you visit department stores, ask the people at the cosmetics counters for free samples, and keep these around the house to be used often.

▶ Even natural supplements can sometimes be contraindicated with certain medications or cause side effects on their own. Ask your senior if she is taking anything like herbs or other supplements. Check them out with her doctor, no matter how harmless you believe they are.

▶ Foot massagers are great for promoting blood circulation.

A digital thermometer is easier to use than a mercury thermometer. Take temperatures using the armpit if your senior has breathing problems or is easily confused.

If Mom has breathing problems and uses an inhaler, keep several around your house and hers, in the car, and so forth.

Many trips to the bathroom may indicate a urinary tract infection, common among seniors who don't always get the fluids they need. Consult a doctor immediately.

Consult a podiatrist immediately for corns, calluses, bunions, blisters, sores and infections, or ingrown, hard, brittle, split, or discolored toenails. If your senior has problem feet, a weekly trip to a salon for a pedicure—for each of you—makes a great outing. Most salons have special discount days plus breaks for seniors. Don't forget to ask about these.

Keep a checklist—a "report card"—and update it periodically to keep track of how your parent is doing with meal preparation, housework, mobility (in and out of the house), laundry, shopping, money issues, medications, bathing, dressing, and eating. These are key activities of daily living (ADLs), and difficulty with them indicates there may be trouble.

If your senior must live in a multilevel home but has problems with stairs, consider a chairlift. They range in price from $2,000 to $20,000. Those prices may sound steep, but they can be cheaper than moving and will help keep your parent independent for a longer time.

For someone who sits a lot, an ergonomic chair that offers greater lumbar support and adjustable features (chair height, armrest height, seat depth) that address particular problems and conditions can be a lifesaver. Ergonomic chairs come in all kinds of models and varying prices. You'll find a good selection and great prices at evofurniture.com; some models are available in every color imaginable, making them an attractive addition to any room.

If an ergonomic chair is not an option, make sure your father's chair has an adjustable height feature, the seat depth is approximately two-thirds the length of his thighs and buttocks, the back is at least fourteen inches high, and the armrests are no more than nine inches high.

Bad posture can complicate back problems and limit mobility. Is Mom walking as upright as she used to? Is Dad favoring one leg over the other for some reason? Sometimes the answer can be as simple as a new pair of shoes.

Osteoporosis is a serious problem for older women, leading to shrinkage and serious (sometimes deadly) fractures. Schedule your senior for a bone density test, and encourage weight-bearing exercise (walking, light weights, gardening). Make sure Mom gets plenty of calcium (the new "chocolate chew" supplements are delicious), and ask her doctor about estrogen replacement therapy.

Make sure Mom is giving herself regular breast exams and that she has a mammogram annually.

If there are precautionary measures that must be remembered, make a checklist and post it in a place where it can't possibly be missed. But change the list and its location from time to time so that it doesn't get taken for granted after a while. If you use a dry erase board or a chalkboard, ask your parent to check off the points as they are followed.

The older you get, the more you are affected by the same amounts of alcohol. On the other hand, a glass of wine now and then has been known to be beneficial for the heart. Check with your loved one's doctor for a good rule of thumb. In the meantime, locate some "zero-proof" recipes and dress them up—tiny umbrellas and all— for a special or even not-so-special occasion.

Don't minimize changes in your parents' health, even if they seem minor. These changes may be accompanied by fear, which can exacerbate even a minor problem. Address your parents' fears; be positive about your ability to find a solution.

Anemia is very common among the elderly, usually resulting from either a loss of blood or a poor diet. Check with the doctor as to whether iron supplements (along with vitamin C, for better absorption) might be in order.

Help prevent infections by keeping antibacterial wet wipes handy at all times. Keep boxes of them around the house; individually wrapped ones can go in your purse or wallet and in the car.

Avoid foot fungus by keeping feet clean and dry. That means changing socks daily and shoes often. It's also a good idea to let feet "air out" once a day.

Nylon or synthetic socks are more likely to make feet sweat. Cotton is better.

If socks are too tight at the tops, they can interfere with circulation. Cut notches into them to make sure they don't bind.

Teach your loved one to respect pain. If something hurts, there's a reason for it.

Bedsores—or pressure sores—result when there is constant pressure on an area where bones are close to the skin's surface. Be on the lookout for problems in these most vulnerable areas: the head, the shoulders, the elbows, the base of the spine, the hips, the heels, and the ankles. Consult a physician if you see red, cracking, or dried skin. In the meantime, encourage Dad to move about when he can, and don't leave him sitting or lying on a damp surface. Make sure linens are not irritating, and wash them often.

Always wear (disposable) rubber gloves when you suspect you might have any kind of skin disorder, such as a rash, an infection, or a lesion of any type.

# EATING

It's a good idea to accompany your mother to the supermarket occasionally to point out new products and to make sure she is shopping wisely. Encourage her to read labels for salt content, sugar, and other health considerations. If she resists, urge her to at least heed fat content. Generally, none of us should be taking in more than 30 percent of our daily calorie intake in the form of fat, and of that, no more than 10 percent should come from saturated fats. Olive oil is a good source of unsaturated fat.

Frozen foods, which are processed right after they are harvested, often retain more vitamins than "fresh" vegetables, which may sit on shelves for days before getting to the supermarket.

When ordering packaged meals from local agencies, ask for extra vegetables. Also, consider supplementing the meal with a homemade side dish.

Would a small refrigerator or a minimicrowave in the bedroom or family room make it easier for Dad to have nutritious snacks all day long?

If shopping is a problem, maybe you can fit an extra freezer in Mom's home somewhere that will allow her to stock up.

▶ Does your grandfather need help with cooking? Contact Meals on Wheels of America (1-703-548-8024 or mealsonwheelsassn.org) to find a local program that will deliver free meals to his home. All seniors older than sixty are eligible. Note that Meals on Wheels doesn't deliver on weekends, so you'll have to make other arrangements. Can a neighbor help? How about a local church or other religious organization? Or ask a local favorite restaurant to deliver a couple of meals.

▶ If your father has vision problems, put liquid in a see-through cup or glass so he can see the liquid.

▶ If your mother's on a special diet, write the day's menu on a blackboard and ask her to check each item off as it's consumed.

▶ Fax a weekly shopping list to your parent's local market and ask for it to be delivered. You can even pay for it over the phone with your credit card.

▶ To find out if your loved one is eligible for food stamps, contact Human Nutrition Services, U.S. Department of Agriculture, 3101 Park Center Drive, Alexandria, VA 22302, 1-703-305-2286.

▶ Find easy recipes that allow your senior to cook with canned and packaged foods—they combine quickly and are quite tasty. There are a variety of cookbooks in this category. Mom might enjoy *Desperation Dinners*, by Beverly Mills and Alicia Ross; for Dad, how about *A Man, a Can, a Plan*, by David Joachim.

▶ There are cookbooks available with easy recipes suitable for special diets (diabetes, heart disease), cooking for one, or microwave cooking. Browse the bookstore or search amazon.com for the one that will suit your senior perfectly.

When you call, casually ask your parent to tell you what he has been eating. "What did you have for dinner last night?" is better than "How's your appetite?"

If Mom is passing up making the meals she once loved because "it's just one person," get her a small wok and a cooking-for-one cookbook. Schedule visits at mealtimes so she'll have an excuse to cook.

If asked, the grocer might break up packages to sell smaller quantities to your senior, like a half-dozen eggs, two potatoes, or just a few slices of bread (the grocer can use the rest of the loaf to make sandwiches).

Ultrapasteurized milk that comes in cardboard cartons has a very long shelf life. Just make sure your parent chills it before drinking and refrigerates it after it's opened.

If your loved one takes a long time to eat, arrange for him to start his meal before everyone else.

Be especially patient at mealtimes; older adults often eat much more slowly than what you may be used to. Try to minimize distractions at mealtimes, and don't bring up stressful subjects.

࿆

"We usually have dinner with my grandmother on Sunday nights. It's nice, but sometimes she can go on autopilot, where instead of having a conversation, she just has a long monologue, a riff on everything. You can't get a word in edgewise. That can be frustrating, but as my father pointed out, she spends a lot of her week alone, bottling up thoughts and ideas, and so when she gets a chance to unload, she needs to let it all out."

—*Ilene Klausner*

A person who is easily confused might have an easier mealtime if you serve one course at a time and clear each one away before serving the next.

A solid-color tablecloth, as opposed to a patterned one, will minimize mealtime distractions.

Maybe your senior just hates eating in the kitchen. Try moving to the dining room or even a space outdoors.

Don't ever wrap dentures in napkins, assuming you will retrieve them after the meal. Chances are they'll be thrown out.

Freeze small containers of your leftovers from home to share with your senior; label them with the date and contents.

Freeze sauces, soups, and bouillon in ice cube trays so that individual servings can be popped out and heated.

Make sure that your senior has access to lots of healthy, easy-to-eat snacks, such as berries, bagels, pitas, cheese, raisins, crackers, energy bars, or apple, melon, or orange slices.

If Mom's appetite is lagging, find out if she has a taste or yen for something special. Experiment with old recipes to make them more palatable and "legal" (use lactose-free milk, salt and sugar substitutes, ground meat instead of cubed, yogurt instead of cream, but first consult a doctor about the interaction of these substitutes with any medications). There are tons of books on the subject and most have recipes. Consult them.

If your loved one is having trouble gaining or maintaining weight, pack his diet with liquid calories. Fruit juices, milk, and milk alternatives such as soy, rice, and nut milks are high in nutrients and calories and are much less filling than solid foods. Smoothies, yogurt shakes, and protein drinks are a little more filling but may still make a good meal alternative.

▸ Respect your father's tastes. If he's hated yogurt all his life, don't start feeding it to him now just because he's less able to resist.

▸ A water filter makes a great gift for a senior.

▸ Four or five smaller meals during the day can be more manageable than three large ones. This approach has the added benefit of keeping blood sugar levels more even throughout the day.

▸ If your parent has vision problems, use the "clock" method of serving food: the main dish is right in front of him at "six o'clock," the starch dish is farthest and directly opposite at "twelve o'clock," and so on.

▸ When family and friends call and ask what gift they can bring, suggest prepared foods. (If your parent gets Meals on Wheels deliveries, save the goodies for the weekend.)

▸ Use plastic bibs at mealtime.

◯◯

"Dad flipped when he saw Mom come at him with a bib! He was furious and refused to wear it. 'I'm not a baby,' he screamed. So the next night when we sat down to eat, all of us—the kids, me, my husband, and his parents—wore bibs. We all wound up laughing about it, and Dad admitted that it wasn't such a big deal after all. We promised never to make him wear it in restaurants, unless, of course, he ordered the lobster."

*—Vonda Giraldo*

It's OK to bring a special meal to a restaurant for your parent and ask to have it microwaved for you, just as long as everyone else is ordering off the menu. Waiters and waitresses want to help you; tell them what you need—privately, to avoid embarrassment. And a good chef, if she's not too busy, can accommodate anyone. Show your appreciation, and tip accordingly.

Dry food can be difficult to swallow. Use sauces generously, but learn to make healthy versions.

Use *flexible* straws.

For those who refuse regular meals, keep healthy snacks (fruits, nutritious cookies, cut-up vegetables) available around the house. Finger foods are best. Be creative—but not overbearing—in your coaxing efforts.

Try using children's nonspill cups with covers or sports drink containers with a straw.

Make mealtime more special by using fancy plates and napkins.

For some, it's easier to cut food with scissors than a knife and fork.

If Mom can't cut her meat any longer, avoid embarrassment by cutting it for her in the kitchen before you serve.

Soft and pureed foods don't have to be bland and tasteless. Find out which herbs and spices make an otherwise bland dish interesting. You might also serve the following in colorful combinations:
- cereal
- puddings and gelatin
- cooked and creamed vegetables
- cheese
- soups and stews

- egg salad and tuna and other fish salads
- tabouli, baba ganoush, and hummus
- cooked fish
- sushi
- pasta
- stewed fruit
- egg rolls, cut up
- chicken nuggets
- scrambled eggs and omelettes
- pancakes and French toast
- rice and risotto
- yogurt
- meat loaf

▶ Baby food is great if you need to get a meal together in a hurry. The fruit selections are delicious!

▶ Get a copy of *The Non-Chew Cookbook*, by Randy J. Wilson; it's available at amazon.com.

▶ No one likes to eat alone. If Mom insists that you partake of her bland, pureed diet, consider bringing along your own snacks at mealtime.

▶ Too many items on the table can be confusing. Keep condiments to a minimum.

∞

---

"My mother hated dinnertime and often refused to settle down for it. So we started a routine of getting a little dressed up for dinner each night—she wears a nice brooch and one of her many scarves, and she likes to carry a purse—and now she looks forward to what's become her favorite part of our day."

—*Michaela Kevis*

Freely make use of microwavable prepackaged foods. You can stock up on them and put them in the freezer after marking each with the day of the week when it should be eaten.

If your loved one can't swallow thin liquids, someone has probably recommended Thick-It, a tasteless powder that thickens hot and cold liquids. The canister is bulky; keep small supplies of Thick-It in your bag to use on outings. If Dad's not supposed to drink unthickened liquid, don't cheat, not even "just this once."

Seniors should always eat sitting up.

Take your parent to lunch, even if you're at work. Call at lunchtime, and you can eat together—you at the desk, she at home in the kitchen. But remember that it's dangerous for an elderly person (or anyone else) to talk while chewing.

Your senior's peak period of digestion (when it's easiest to digest food) is midday. Plan the large meal for that time of day, and keep supper light.

When feeding your father, only put one teaspoon of food in his mouth at once. Alternate spoonfuls of solids and liquids.

Plan your mother's weekly menu ahead of time so shopping for all meals can be done at once. Copy her recipes onto cards and write the shopping list for each dish on the backs. Take the cards with you when you go shopping.

Seniors who seem to have endless appetites often forget they have just eaten. Put stickers on the clock for mealtimes so they can see how long it is until the next meal. Making small nutritious snacks available throughout the day is also helpful.

▶ Your senior should never lie down right after a meal—that is the most common cause of indigestion. (Eating too fast is the second most common cause.) Make sure Mom sits or stands for at least an hour after she eats.

▶ Many medications leave an awful taste in the mouth that is far worse than anything you can imagine. They can make sugar taste like salt, and some favorite foods become completely inedible. Be especially patient during this time as you try new things to see what works. In the meantime, a lollipop may help your loved one after he's eaten something distasteful. (Don't give sucking candies to anyone who might easily swallow them whole.)

▶ You can get someone to come to the house just to feed meals to your parent. Contact your Area Agency on Aging.

▶ Even if Mom isn't making use of the local senior center, she can attend every day just for meals.

▶ If salt is an issue, there are a bunch of flavorful seasoning substitutes on the market.

෬෨

---

"I *bribed* Mom to eat toward the end—it was the only way I could get her to take anything. I actually gave her a quarter for every meal. The funny thing is, I forgot all about this. Then, after she passed away and we were going through her bedroom, I found jars of quarters under her bed! It all added up to over $150, which we donated to the local food bank, which is exactly where I knew she'd want it to go. It helped give us closure to know that the money that helped feed our mother would now feed others."

—*Brenda Bienvenuti*

There are tons of special utensils that can make eating a lot easier; a combination fork and knife for one-handed eating, a tilted spoon for someone with hand problems, or a two-handled mug for easier drinking are available from the many suppliers of special-needs items. You can also buy plate guards that keep food from sliding off. B Independent (1-913-390-0247 or bindependent.com) offers a wide range of such products.

Jews, Sikhs, Muslims, and Hindus all incorporate fasting into various rituals and celebrations. If your parent is observant but you suspect he may not be physically up to the fast, speak to his doctor or his minister, who can talk to him about reasonable exemptions from fasting.

Diet supplements like Ensure are widely used in hospitals and nursing homes. Keep them cooled. Put a few cans on ice in the morning, and make them available all day long.

A glass of wine, if it's not contraindicated for other reasons, can stimulate the appetite.

## SLEEP

If Grandma has trouble sleeping (and is not bedridden), encourage her to spend as little "awake time" as possible in bed. Reading, watching TV, and so forth, should be done in a favorite chair, while bed is for sleep only. Going to sleep and waking up at about the same time each day will also help train her body for better sleep overall.

Seniors should avoid oversleeping in the morning. It leads to having trouble falling asleep later, and the cycle of insomnia begins.

If Dad can't fall asleep within fifteen minutes of getting into bed, suggest he get up for a while and do something calming, and then try again later.

Don't take sleep disruption lightly. It can be caused by an improper dose of medication, an illness, or a psychological problem. Talk about it with your loved one's doctor. Many drugs, including Halcyon and even the antidepressants that are supposed to make her life better, can cause terrifying nightmares.

If your father wakes with night terrors, be reassuring. Show him that there's no danger nearby but avoid arguing. If he insists that something (or someone) woke him, let him know that whatever the trouble was, it's gone now.

People of any age who have difficulty sleeping should avoid exercise in the late afternoon and evening. Try morning walks instead.

Avoid caffeine not just in the evening but at any time of day. Aside from coffee, tea, and cola, look out for caffeine in chocolate, non-cola soft drinks, and some pain relievers. And while decaffeinated coffee has less caffeine than regular, it's not caffeine-free.

Alcohol can make your senior drowsy at first, but it hurts healthy sleep in the long run by disturbing the sleep cycle, making sleep less restful, and making him more likely to wake up during the night.

⚬⚬

As with practically everything, "A good laugh and a long sleep are the two best cures."

—*Irish proverb*

Maintain a sleep diary to note sleep patterns. The doctor will find this information useful if you need to consult with her, and you might discover patterns you weren't aware of: Is sleeping a problem the night before the family comes to visit? Is this about anxiety or excitement? Get a free sleep diary from the National Sleep Foundation by calling 1-202-347-3471.

If there are serious issues that require discussion, don't bring these up right before bedtime. Avoid arguments.

Some people swear by a teaspoon of honey in a cup of hot water before bedtime. Others go for warm milk with a little cinnamon. But if liquids are a problem before bed, find a different solution. A foot bath or massage right before bed can help.

Get dark-lined (blackout) shades for people who don't sleep well, and block out disturbing noise with a fan or a white noise machine. Some models have a choice of sounds that mimic ocean waves, the patter of raindrops, and other soothing sounds.

Aromatherapy using lavender candles and potpourri can be very relaxing. Try a couple drops of lavender oil in a bath or on the corner of your senior's pillow. You can even buy a microwavable teddy bear filled with potpourri that stays warm and aromatic for hours after a short "nap" in the microwave. These come in two sizes from ThermiPaq. Visit their website at thermipaq.com, call them at 1-800-800-5728, or write to them at ThermiPaq, Thermionics Corporation, 3501 South Sixth Street, Springfield, IL 62703. Also check out their line of other pain relief and relaxation products.

Change the linens often. Everyone enjoys fresh sheets. You can even buy lavender water to put in the wash! It's sold in a lot of home stores and catalogs these days.

Unpleasant odors can interfere with sleep. Use potpourri and make sure the air in the room has a chance to circulate. When Mom's out of the room for a while, open the windows or light a scented candle.

Create a sleep ritual before bedtime and follow this every evening. If you live far away, you can still call at bedtime to wish your parents sweet dreams.

Cotton pajamas and sheets are less irritating than synthetics.

Restless leg syndrome is a condition in which one leg or both legs experience nervous sensations that cause excessive movement. It's a fairly common condition that can often be treated with medication, iron supplements, and exercise. Is this what's keeping your loved one awake? Find out more online and talk to your doctor.

Does Dad's snoring rock the house? Is Grandma really sleepy in the morning and drowsy during the day? They may have sleep apnea, a disorder in which the person stops breathing at points during sleep. Consistent loud snoring and morning and daytime sleepiness are some of the warning signs. Men, people who are over forty, and people who are overweight are all at higher risk, but anyone can have it, and it's more common than diabetes. Sleep apnea can lead to insomnia, high blood pressure, weight gain, headaches, memory problems, excessive drowsiness, depression, impotence—the list goes on. The good news is that it can be treated, so talk to the doctor or contact the American Sleep Apnea Association (1-202-293-3650 or sleepapnea.org).

Make sure the mattress your father sleeps on is comfortable and right for him. Soft beds are nice, but maybe he needs more support. It's easier to rise from a firm mattress.

▶ Some people are just not morning people. If getting your parent up every morning is a problem and you already have enough to do at that hour, let her stay in bed until midmorning, if she likes, and get her up after the family has gone off to work and school.

▶ While it may be tempting to take naps, they should be avoided if they interfere with getting a good night's sleep.

▶ Arrange calming activities before bedtime; this is a time for reading, soft music, and soothing conversation. Have your loved one spend some time in pajamas before settling in to sleep.

▶ Saying prayers together before bedtime can be a wonderful ritual.

▶ Maybe Mom can't sleep because she has issues she can't talk about. Try to discuss this with her, or suggest she discuss the problem with another member of the family or a professional.

▶ Remind your senior to go to the bathroom before going to sleep. If he gets up often at night to go to the bathroom, suggest that he doesn't drink any liquids for three or four hours before bedtime. On the other hand, don't skimp too much on fluids because you want to cut down on bathroom visits. Seniors often become dehydrated, which leads to painful (but common) urinary tract infections.

▶ Learn sleep techniques and teach them to your senior:
  ■ Listen to your own breath and count breaths. Get comfortable, close your eyes, and begin breathing slowly but normally, then count each exhalation, either starting at one or counting back from one hundred.
  ■ Practice progressive muscle relaxation by tensing and relaxing one limb at a time. Make a fist and clench your right arm, while keeping the left relaxed; then relax the right arm. Repeat with the left arm, then each leg.

- Use visualization techniques to picture yourself in a perfect, relaxing place, such as a quiet beach or lakeside.
- Try a tape or CD that will guide you through a relaxation exercise or visualization. We like *Total Relaxation*, by John Harvey, but there are many available. You can even make your own.
- Make up for lost sleep as soon as possible.

A baby monitor will alert you to any nighttime problems your parent may be having, and he will feel secure knowing that if he calls in the middle of the night, you will hear him. Show him how the monitor works.

If it's the bed that's keeping your father awake, consider getting a hospital bed. Medicare will pay for it if his doctor recommends it.

A foam "egg crate" mattress will help prevent bedsores and can be purchased from any medical supply house.

Rotate a new mattress once a month the first year and every season (four times a year) after that. A mattress should be replaced every eight to ten years.

If they sleep in the same bed but Mom needs a firm mattress and Dad prefers something softer, consider getting two single beds and moving them next to each other. You can use king- or queen-sized bedding, so it looks like one bed. This allows many couples to feel comfortable without giving up intimacy.

A clock with brightly illuminated numbers can keep someone awake. Use the dimmer on the clock if it has one, turn the clock to the wall, or get a new clock.

Some people have trouble sleeping because their biological clocks are waking them at weird times. To "reset" Dad's biological clock, have him get up in the morning at the time he's like to awaken each day and spend about ten minutes facing the sun.

If your mother grinds her teeth at night—a common condition called bruxism—talk to the dentist. Mom might need a mouth guard.

Keep familiar, favorite photos at the bedside to calm Mom in case she wakes up confused about where she is. If she travels or has to spend some time in the hospital, keep these same items at her bedside there for continuity.

For information about sleep disorders, consult the American Sleep Disorders Association, 604 Second Street SW, Rochester, MN 55902.

## EXERCISE

Nowhere is the saying "use it or lose it" more meaningful than among seniors. Aside from its cardiovascular benefits, exercise combats depression and osteoporosis, reduces the risk of falling, cuts down on healing time when there are injuries and illnesses, and generally improves lifestyle. Encourage your grandmother to stick to a routine.

Ask your senior to keep an exercise log and consult it often. Compliment his progress and celebrate breakthroughs.

Yoga is a great form of gentle exercise that improves the immune system and promotes well-being, among many other benefits. Weight training, Tai Chi, swimming, and low-impact aerobics are also generally beneficial to seniors.

Make your own exercise video for your mother. She might hate the idea of staring at a nubile twenty-something while she does her stretching exercises, but what if, instead, she had an image of you or her granddaughter guiding her through the routine? If you own a video camera, don't pass up this opportunity to make each day more special for her.

Set up an area of your senior's home where he can exercise safely. Make it special: get an attractive exercise mat and maybe even hang up an inspirational poster. Get him colorful workout wear or a funny T-shirt ("Over the hill? What hill?").

If you can't go yourself, hire a reliable teen to take your parent for a walk. The outing might be less awkward if you give it a purpose, like a daily trip to the store for bagels and a newspaper.

Gardening, housecleaning, and shopping can be considered exercise. Redefine the word *exercise* as needed.

Things change. From time to time, review your loved one's exercise routine to make sure it's still appropriate.

Encourage deep breathing. Most people forget to breathe when they exercise.

Check with a doctor or physical therapist before your loved one embarks on any exercise routine.

৩৩

"I've heard that advice about a million times and was assured by our family doctor that Dad's calisthenics were just fine for him. But it never occurred to me to check back after he developed a minor ear infection that left him with a slight balancing problem. It turned out that even some of the neck rolls he was doing were affecting his ability to stand up without getting dizzy."

—*Bari Meyer*

If your grandfather isn't motivated to exercise, take him to a ball game to remind him of what it was like to have the wind blow through his hair (when he had hair). Walking to your seats is enough to get the body moving, and the fresh air will do wonders for him.

Bring your senior to a physical therapist for advice and general guidance. If you can get Dad's doctor to recommend the visit, insurance will pay for it. If not, it'll be a worthy expense, given the possible benefits.

All exercise routines, even walking, should start and end with a period of stretching. A stretch needs to be held for at least five seconds to be effective.

If your father refuses to exercise, try to get him to at least work on one of the important muscle groups: arms, legs, shoulders, or back.

Exercising to music is always more fun, especially if the music is your favorite. Make your loved one a special exercise tape of his favorite tunes.

If your senior totally resists the idea of exercise, don't try to bully her into it. Request a copy of the free booklet *Pep Up Your Life: A Fitness Book for Seniors* from AARP by calling 1-800-424-3410.

The mall opens before the stores do, and in many areas, people have discovered that they're a great place to walk. Aisles are nice and wide, and it's temperature controlled year-round. It's also a great way to meet people. Make sure security has arrived on duty by the time your senior gets there.

Exercise reduces stress. That's probably something you both need. Do it together.

Consider a professional personal trainer. Even if it's too expensive to have one regularly, a couple sessions will get your senior started on the right track and allow her to develop an appropriate routine.

It's a good idea for someone else to be around when your senior exercises, just in case there are problems. If you or a family member can't be there, this is a potential job for a responsible teen.

An hour of brisk walking four times a week can drastically improve the quality of life for a senior—or anyone else, for that matter.

Buy Mom a pedometer so she can measure her distance when she walks.

Start a senior exercise class in your dad's neighborhood. A small group can pool their resources and hire a teacher just for them, at their convenience. If no one has a basement big enough, ask restaurant owners whether their private rooms, which are rarely used during the daytime, can be made available. Or perhaps the local school can let them use part of the gym when it's not being used.

Walking is still the best exercise there is. Learn to enjoy walking slowly with your loved one.

☙

"When I first started taking Gramps out for short walks, I thought I'd go crazy—each block took a good half hour, which was often the length of a whole visit. I soon learned to appreciate the value of slowing down my day this way, and seeing the world this way brought us closer together."

—*Steve Fein*

Yoga classes can be beneficial to both you and your loved one. Consider taking classes together.

If your parent hates the idea of walking, ask him to help you by running certain errands for you ("Dad, could you be a doll and return this to the library for me?").

Swimming is often an option for seniors who have lost mobility. Also, water exercise classes are available at many swimming facilities.

Dancing: it's good exercise, it's a great social activity, the music can be therapeutic, and it's a wonderful way to meet people. Find out what classes are available locally, and don't ignore those classes that are aimed at kids. Instructors at those classes might be willing to start offering adult classes if enough students can be gathered. Plant the idea—swing your partner!

Look into special senior exercise programs in the neighborhood. Visit the classes on your own before you suggest your parent joins. There are some good ones out there, but some can be depressing to those who are fairly vital.

Squeezing balls of clay is good exercise for arthritic hands, as are therapeutic squeeze balls made just for that purpose. They're available at most drugstores.

Seniors have found that weight lifting using relatively light weights strengthens the body, helps bone density, increases flexibility, and reassures them of their abilities.

*Always* check with a doctor before your loved one embarks on any exercise program.

# 6

# Common Infirmities

ᦉ

## DEPRESSION

▶Depression is the most common psychological problem among people of all ages, including the elderly. Common symptoms are:
- lack of interest in activities that used to be enjoyable
- lack of energy
- social withdrawal
- feelings of hopelessness
- strong feelings of guilt or self-criticism
- eating less or more than usual and losing or gaining weight
- sleeping less or more than usual
- difficulty concentrating

▶Depression is not "normal" in the elderly. While it may seem natural for older people to be sad due to loss, loneliness, and so forth, sadness and depression aren't the same thing, and many seniors experience these problems without becoming depressed. It's an illness in the elderly just like in other age groups. *And* it's treatable. Don't assume your loved one's depression is "just old age"—get help.

Some depressed people, particularly older folks, may experience a lot of physical symptoms such as headaches, digestive trouble, and bodily aches and pains. Don't make assumptions about where the symptoms are coming from, but consider that these symptoms may be caused or aggravated by depression.

People who are depressed feel that way because they can't help it. Trying to talk your senior out of his depression won't work, and lecturing him on all the things he has to be thankful for will only make him feel guilty. It's a better idea to listen and tell him you know how he feels and that perhaps tomorrow will be better.

Advances in the treatment of depression are relatively new, and your senior may not be aware of just how treatable this disease is. Talk to her about medical advances, and pass along news articles on the subject when you come across them. Don't bring up the subject next time you see her; give her the space to think about it at her own pace.

Depression can be a little different in older people than it is in others. For example, many seniors find that they have difficulty crying and expressing emotion as they get older. Get to know the many faces of depression.

ि

"It took a while for me to figure out that Dad was depressed, because he never seemed sad and I didn't see him cry once. He just got very quiet, had very little energy, and didn't seem interested in any of his hobbies—I just thought he was tired. I don't think even he knew what was going on until someone at the senior center gave a talk about depression, and he admitted that he had been having a lot of hopeless thoughts and had even thought about suicide. Once we realized what the problem was, we were able to do something about it."

—*Keesha Varick*

Exercise, such as walking for thirty minutes three to four times a week, has been shown to decrease depression in the elderly as well as other age groups.

Enjoyable activities of any kind are a good relief for depression. Unfortunately it's hard for a depressed person to get started with them. Be gently encouraging and try to make manageable activity (short walks, movies, games, social visits) available to a depressed loved one.

Grief is a natural reaction to loss. A grieving person experiences many of the symptoms of depression, but this is normal unless the person has suicidal thoughts or feelings of worthlessness or if other symptoms don't start to improve after two months. In any of these cases, get professional help.

Give your senior the time and space he needs to grieve for a loved one, but after a few weeks begin to *gently* encourage him to social- ize, resume hobbies, and so on. Don't expect him to snap back to normal right away, but don't let him sit alone in a dark room either.

Suicide rates are high in the sixty-five and older age group. If your loved one is depressed or mentions suicide, death, or hopelessness, get help immediately.

Take any mention of suicide seriously. Do not promise to keep the conversation a secret.

If you're at all concerned about suicide, consider making a written agreement with your senior in which she promises to tell you if she has thoughts about hurting herself, and you promise not to freak out if she tells you. Both of you should sign the agreement. Just remember that you can't be her therapist—get professional help if she admits to having suicidal thoughts.

Chronic physical illness and disability can lead to depression. At the same time, depression and some physical illnesses have symptoms in common, so one may look like the other. Try to keep your mind open to this relationship when caring for your loved one, especially if there is difficulty pinpointing a problem or finding a solution.

Older generations are less comfortable with the idea of psychotherapy and talking about psychological issues. Be sensitive to this difference when dealing with your loved one.

If your senior really hates the idea of paying someone, maybe he'd feel more comfortable in a neighborhood support group.

Teach the other family members about what depression is (and isn't). Tell them the best ways to show their support. If you object to anything they do, tell them privately.

Recognize that everyone is different, and therefore individual experiences with depression are different. Don't assume you know how someone feels just because you've been depressed yourself.

༄༅

"I took Mom to a shrink once—and only once—after which she pulled the young doctor aside and said, 'Tell me, is your job to sit here and ask questions all day?' He said it was. 'And they pay you for this?' she asked incredulously. When he replied that yes, he was paid, and that we now owed him $175 for the forty-five-minute session, my mother wrote him a check, went home, and has been smiling ever since. Her traditional upbringing through near-poverty taught her that only rich people have time for depression. That's the way she was brought up, and that's the way she's determined to live her life. Even if I tell her that insurance will pay the fee, she still doesn't buy it."

—*Fay Solomon*

▶ When discussing antidepressants with your parents, know their side effects. Don't downplay sexual dysfunction, which is a common side effect. If it's a concern to them, respect that and point to drugs that won't interfere with their sex lives. (Yes, there's a good chance they're still "doing it"!)

▶ Many people swear by Saint-John's-wort, a natural remedy that supposedly combats depression, among other ailments. But medical studies show that if it has any effect at all, it's far slower and less potent than prescription medications. And like any other "natural remedies," it has side effects and possible harmful interactions with other drugs.

▶ Antidepressant medications work well for many people but can take a while (sometimes months) to have an effect. Make sure Dad doesn't give up on taking them just because they don't start working right away. On the other hand, sometimes the dosage needs to be adjusted or the medication needs to be changed. Ask the doctor how long it might take for the drug to take effect. In the meantime, if you notice any adverse reaction (e.g., irritability, nightmares), discontinue the medication *and* contact the doctor immediately.

▶ Antidepressants aren't like cold medicine. People can't just stop taking the pills when they feel better. Discontinuing any psychotropic medication should be supervised by a physician because suddenly stopping can cause a rebound effect—in which the person feels worse!

▶ Lose the booze. While alcohol can be a temporary comfort, it actually makes depression worse.

▶ It helps for some people to put their feelings down on paper; encourage your mother to keep a journal and assure her it will stay private. Or maybe she'd rather keep an audio journal by talking into a tape recorder.

Depression is a common side effect of many drugs typically taken by the elderly, including Valium, Xanax, Lopressor, Norpace, Zantac, Tagamet, Dilantin, and Advil. Even some antidepressants can have the opposite effect.

A therapy group is a great place for your loved one to share her feelings with peers who can possibly relate to her better than you can, at least in regard to a specific problem. Seek out groups that address themselves to your mother's particular situation. Special groups for Holocaust and disaster survivors, for singles, or based on ethnic background can be located through your local Area Agency on Aging.

Find out more about depression and locate local doctors and support groups by contacting the National Foundation for Depressive Illness (1-800-248-4344) or the National Mental Health Association (1-800-969-6642 or nmha.org). You can also get information about depression (and other disorders) from the National Institute of Mental Health (1-301-443-4513 or nimh.nih.gov).

If your father loses his appetite during this tough time, don't force the issue by trying to entice him with elaborate meals he can't enjoy. It will make him feel guilty and even sadder. Keep the meals simple—sandwiches and one-dish meals—until the feelings pass.

Just listen. Use body language to communicate patience when Dad tells you how he feels. Face him straight on, sit at his level, and maintain eye contact.

## MEMORY AND DEMENTIA

The saying "use it or lose it" applies to mental exercise as well as physical. Encourage activities that keep the mind sharp:
- card games
- crossword puzzles

- trivia games (adjust the questions to the appropriate level of your senior; look in the children's section of the bookstore for fun books with thousands of questions)
- word-finding games
- jigsaw puzzles
- board games (your six-year-old might finally have found someone who is willing to sit through endless games of Candyland!)

If you're giving your senior directions or information like a phone number or an address, ask her to repeat it back to you so you know she's understood you correctly. Don't get impatient if she doesn't get it right the first—or third—time.

Don't give too much detail that may get in the way of what you really need to communicate. When telling a complicated story, tell a simple version of it first, and then go back and embellish parts you need to. Let your loved one know the overall point of the story before you tell it.

Be specific when communicating with your senior. "Would you like to go shopping now or after lunch?" is better than "When do you want to go shopping?"

Establish permanent places for objects that are often misplaced; insist on consistency here.

Look out for the most common signs of dementia:
- memory loss—forgetting names, dates, and so on
- confusion—losing the thread in the middle of a story
- disorientation—trouble keeping track of the day, the time, or one's location
- problems with self-care—poor grooming, not eating properly
- mood swings—especially unpredictable irritability
- language problems—difficulty finding words in conversation

- math difficulty—problems calculating a tip at a restaurant
- poor judgment—like making a left turn in front of an oncoming car

▶ It's normal for people to experience a *very gradual* decline in learning and memory as they get older. But if there has been any noticeable change for your senior in the areas just described, *don't* assume it's merely normal aging—get her evaluated.

▶ Don't constantly correct a faulty memory. Ask yourself if it's really important before you do. Maybe the factual details aren't as meaningful as the subject under discussion and Mom's pride in being able to tell the story.

☾☽

"It used to bother me when my mother would remember things incorrectly. She'd get dates and lots of other things mixed up, and I was always correcting her. Once she started telling a whole story about how I broke my leg in summer camp, when in fact it had been my brother. I sort of jumped in midsentence to set her straight, and she looked at me and just got quiet. Later my twelve-year-old said, 'Dad, does it really matter *that much* which one of you broke a leg in camp? Are the fact police going to come in and arrest us?' That was a reality check for me. I realized it was more important that she enjoy her memories, even if they weren't exactly accurate, and that we enjoy our time together without unnecessary tension. I also realized that I'm a little uptight about my own memory, and I worry that I won't remember things well when I get older. It actually inspired me to start writing down some memories about our family and my own younger years. It also made me glad to know that my son, who's apparently much wiser in these matters than I, will be patient with me when my own facts aren't all that straight."

*—Jim Bamberger*

▶ Because the two have some symptoms in common (like difficulty concentrating and remembering), depression is sometimes mistaken for dementia in the elderly and vice versa. Make sure Dad is screened for both. Also, make sure you don't confuse hearing problems with dementia.

▶ There's more than one kind of dementia, and each kind has very different prognoses and treatment options, so it's important to find out exactly what your senior is dealing with. Some kinds of dementia (like those related to drug reactions or thyroid problems) can be reversible if detected early.

▶ The most common type of dementia is Alzheimer's disease (AD). If your senior has AD, contact the National Alzheimer's Association (1-800-272-3900 or alz.org), which has a wealth of information and resources available.

▶ Avoid quizzing: "Do you know what day it is?" "Do you remember where we lived?" "Do you know who I am?" Chances are your senior will find this line of interrogation both annoying and belittling.

▶ Old habits die hard; respect them.

◎

"For as long as I can remember, Dad started every day with a cup of coffee and the newspaper. I don't think we were even allowed to talk to him until he'd gotten to the sports section. Dad can no longer read, but he sure does love to stare at the paper for about an hour every morning. I have no idea what goes through his mind when he does this, but I could swear that this favorite ritual makes just a little part of him feel 'normal' again."

—Sam Trumball

If your confused senior isn't in the mood to sort something out, let it go.

Too many choices can overwhelm someone who is only slightly confused. To make dressing easier, divide a large closet into two smaller ones, and hang only a few of your mother's garments in one of them. Hang socks and underwear on hangers with clothespins to make finding them easier. In the kitchen, put all often-used items in one cupboard so she doesn't even have to worry or think about the other cupboards.

Casually keep Mom informed as to what's going on around her: "Good morning, Mom. What a beautiful Sunday morning this is." "Oh, look, here come Bob and Terry." "It's snowing—just in time for Christmas next week."

The Safe Return Program, sponsored by the National Alzheimer's Association, provides bracelets and necklaces with identification that will enable your loved one's safe return if she wanders off or gets lost. The program has saved more than six thousand lives since its inception in 1993, and it's fairly inexpensive: $40 to register and $5 for each bracelet. Consult your local Alzheimer's Association or visit alz.org/resourcecenter/programs/safereturn.htm.

Create simple mnemonic devices to help your loved one remember things.

&

"Gramps remembers our special code—LOW—before he leaves the house. He checks that the **L**ights are off, the **O**ven is turned off, and the **W**indows are shut."

—*Inez Guarina*

Boundaries made of flowers, hedges, or garden ornaments are "friend-lier" than forbidding fences and may accomplish the same purpose.

Never leave a memory-impaired person alone in a parked car.

If you need to hang signs on doors so your loved one will be able to identify the room, use a picture, not just a word for the sign; for example, the bedroom sign might have a picture of a bed, while the bathroom sign should have a photo of a toilet.

People who are likely to wander should always carry identification—consider an ID bracelet. Also keep a recent photo of your senior available in case the police ever need to search for him.

If your senior is agitated, try to find out why instead of telling him to calm down. Is he in pain? Is he frightened? Too cold? Hungry? There's usually a reason, even if it's one that he's overreacting to.

If a confused person insists on searching for something, even if the object is imaginary, help her look for it.

When talking to a confused person, try to establish eye contact, which makes communication easier. Supplement verbal messages with gestures and facial expressions that communicate meaning.

Seniors often wander at night because they are restless. They may need exercise before bedtime.

☙

"We found the nighttime wandering episodes declining once we started taking Dad out for a nice long walk before he went to bed."

—*Aggie Cline*

A person with dementia will often "shadow" you (follow you around the house) or call or come looking for you five minutes after you've told him you're going to fold the laundry. This can get pretty frustrating. You can make a set of index cards on which are written cues such as "Sarah is in the basement doing laundry" or "Mike is taking a nap upstairs." Teach Dad to look in a specific place (his shirt pocket, on top of the TV) when he's confused about where you might be, and place the proper card there before you go. This really works!

Try to repeat key words in your sentences: "I'm going out now, *out*." "I'll tell you when the doctor calls. The *doctor* will *call*."

A confused person can more easily understand what you want him to do than he can understand what you *don't* want him to do. "Let's watch TV" is better than "Don't touch that."

Seniors are often confused when they awaken and are not sure if it's daytime or nighttime. Get a clock that indicates A.M. or P.M.

Those suffering from dementia often hoard objects such as food and other household items. Check common hiding places often.

_____

"Mom's Alzheimer's caused her to become a 'hoarder.' There didn't seem to be any rhyme or reason to what she hoarded, but almost daily I would find food under her bed, batteries in her purse, and my magazines stuffed into shoe boxes on the floor of her closet. Our social worker suggested that designating one closet as her own might make her feel 'safe' and therefore less prone to stocking up. It didn't work. She still hoards. But at least I don't have to go running all over the place to look for my things. They all wind up in Mom's closet."

—*Jill Marcinczuk*

Don't whisper or talk about your senior in the third person when he's present. People with dementia are prone to paranoia and might believe that you're plotting against them. Also, it's rude.

Don't lay out clothing the night before. A confused person is liable to get up in the middle of the night and get dressed, thinking it's morning.

If your mother's agitated when you leave and forgets when you'll return, put a small colored sticky tag or a small piece of clay on the clock to show when you're coming back.

If you must install locks on doors to keep your senior safe, she may feel "trapped" once she realizes she can't leave on her own. Try installing the lock either high up or low down so seeing it isn't a constant reminder of her confinement. Avoid locks that require a key or a combination. In an emergency, there may not be time to hunt for the key or figure out the combination.

If your senior is fussing and being more uncooperative than usual, check to see if any environmental factors may be causing a problem. Is there noise or commotion outside that may be distracting or annoying? Is the lighting sufficient? Is it too bright?

ᦆ

"When Dad gets especially nasty, I'll sometimes distract him by drastically changing the light in the room. If it's morning and the curtains haven't been opened yet, I find that the flood of sunlight when I open them changes his mood almost instantly. I also notice that he hates fluorescent lights, which glare and I think he associates with hospitals. He gets very uneasy when we go into stores with strong fluorescent lighting."

—*Roberta Mallia*

If Dad wanders often, let the neighbors know and ask them to alert you if they see him alone.

Add clamps or dowels to windows, allowing them to open wide enough to let in fresh air but not wide enough for a person to fit through. Hardware stores sell various devices made for just this purpose.

Hang attractive jingle bells, nestled against a bouquet of dried flowers, on the backs of doors so you can hear when the door is opened without drawing attention to the need for security.

Those who suffer from dementia and repeatedly ask which plate is theirs would benefit from having their own set of plates in a special color that are always identifiable as theirs.

Keep a log of your senior's behavior, especially any dramatic episodes. You may discover a pattern.

Be gentle when you refer to events in the past that have upset your senior. People with dementia often relive the experience every time the subject comes up.

૭๏

"I think the saddest part was when Mom repeatedly asked why Dad didn't come to see her. When I reminded her that he had passed away two years ago, she'd react as though she was hearing it for the first time. And then she would get upset with me for not telling her sooner. Now when she asks where Dad is, I tell her he's home, resting, and that seems to be the end of it. We avoid the drama, and technically, I'm not lying."

—*Maureen Funsch*

Often, people with dementia view a black floor as an impassable abyss. To discourage someone from entering certain rooms or leaving the house, place a black rug or doormat on the floor.

Electronic devices that alert you to movement in a room are commonly used to monitor infants. They can help you keep an eye on your senior as well.

"Sundowning" is a state of increased agitation that occurs in dementia patients late in the day through the evening. If your loved one exhibits this pattern, make a point of setting aside the period just before sundowning for either a nap or some other quiet, relaxing activity. This is a good time to just sit next to her while you each do something independently, perhaps with some soft music playing. If she enjoys having you read to her, this is the perfect time for it. Also, increasing artificial light in the late afternoon and early evening can reduce the agitation. If sundowning is particularly troublesome, consult your loved one's doctor.

If you've been snapping at Mom and now understand that she suffers from dementia, forgive yourself and think about ways in which you can show more patience now that you're more aware of what's happening.

## HEARING LOSS

Hearing loss can be very gradual and hard to notice—or admit—for many of us. Have hearing checked regularly, and look for symptoms of deterioration:
- very high volume on the television or radio
- asking people to repeat things
- appearing to ignore questions

- becoming angry when questioned
- withdrawing from conversation
- difficulty with or avoiding the telephone
- ringing in the ears

A person with hearing difficulty will often simply nod or otherwise agree to questions or comments he can't hear to avoid trouble or embarrassment. Make sure you're not just being "yessed."

A sudden hearing problem may be caused by a buildup of earwax. Consult a doctor. He may remove the wax himself, or he might prescribe ear drops that will dissolve it.

Dad might not even know that he has a hearing problem. Maybe he's acting withdrawn and depressed because he thinks he's getting senile, when the real problem is that he can't hear what's being said to him. This is one of those times when communication and a watchful eye can save the day.

When speaking with someone with hearing difficulty, talking loudly just distorts your voice. Instead, speak slowly and clearly, facing the listener. Avoid covering your mouth.

Eliminate background noise when you're talking to someone with a hearing problem. The radio, a lawn mower, or other voices can make hearing impossible.

Make sure you know how Mom's hearing aid works. Check to see that it is working properly, and insert fresh batteries when they're needed. You also need to know how to insert the hearing aid in her ear. This can be tricky. It's a good idea to accompany Mom to the doctor when she's fitted for the hearing aid.

Electronic hearing aids that don't require batteries, and which automatically adjust sound levels, are more expensive but worth it if you can afford them. On the other hand, you don't want one that has more features than you need. All hearing aids should come with warranties, and there should be a thirty-day free trial period during which you can return the hearing aid for a full refund or just a small service charge. If this is not the way the supplier works, shop elsewhere. Compare prices—they vary greatly.

Keep a supply of extra hearing aid batteries handy at all times. Keep them in the car in case of emergencies, in your purse, and so forth.

Most insurance plans don't cover the cost of hearing aids. But Medi-gap insurance, available through AARP, does.

Attach hearing aids to clothing using alligator clips. Ask the doctor to order these special attachments at the time the hearing aid is ordered.

It generally takes about six weeks to get used to a new hearing aid.

If Mom is embarrassed by her hearing aid, suggest a hairstyle that covers it. Or get her a nice hat.

If your father is hearing impaired, always approach him from the front, where he can see you. Get his attention by touching him gently and saying his name.

Make sure you have your hearing-impaired senior's attention before you start communicating. Speak slowly and introduce the subject: "About the party tomorrow . . ."

People with hearing impairments are often extremely shy and embarrassed about letting anyone else know. Let your father know how widespread hearing problems are and that they have become "socially acceptable." Urge him to alert his friends to the problem so they can make adjustments when they speak and socialize.

Avoid sudden changes in topic. If the subject of the conversation changes, introduce it slowly: "Now let's talk about our trip to the country."

To make a room comfortable for a hearing-impaired person, there should be carpeting on the floor and other sound-absorbing fixtures. Chairs should not be too far apart but not too close either. Three feet between chairs is just about right.

Medical supply companies sell small microphones that amplify conversations in small areas, such as a small room or the car.

Most movies and theaters offer assisted-listening devices (headphones) for free or at a nominal cost. Headphones are also useful at home for listening to the stereo or TV.

Ask your cable provider about closed captioning and other devices for the hearing impaired, such as headphones and audio enhancers.

Telephone conversations can be difficult for people with even a slight hearing problem. Ask the telephone company about TDD (telecommunications devices for the deaf).

When you're speaking with your senior over the phone, don't invite other members of the family to pick up an extension and join the conversation. It will be more difficult for your parent to hear each of you.

A speech therapist can teach anyone basic lip-reading skills. This will be covered by insurance if a doctor prescribes it.

A dog could be a wonderful companion for your father if he's hard of hearing. The dog could alert Dad to a doorbell he can't hear, to people approaching, or to a ringing telephone. There are dogs specially trained for this purpose, but any well-trained dog would be helpful.

Get your hearing-impaired senior a vibrating pager. There are also alarm clocks that vibrate the bed when they go off and flashing devices as well. You'll find a great selection of these at seniorshops.com or Assistive Devices Network (1-866-674-3549 or assistivedevices.net).

Even a slight hearing problem can affect a person's ability to drive safely. Drive with your parent often to make sure his skills are up to snuff.

A person who can't hear well will get special enjoyment from the ability to send E-mail to friends and family.

It's easiest for a hearing-impaired person to enjoy a conversation at a round table than one that's oblong or square.

Put important messages and notes in writing. Fax machines are especially helpful in households where hearing loss makes phone conversations difficult.

Install smoke alarms that employ a strong strobe light in addition to sound. Install one in each room.

Try to engage your hearing-impaired senior in visually oriented amusements: a birdhouse or ant colony, people watching, and so forth.

## Vision Loss

Look for the common warning signs of failing vision:
- trouble adjusting to dark rooms
- squinting or blinking due to sensitivity to light

- double vision
- swollen or irritated eyelids
- seeing dark spots, "floaters," or cloudiness
- loss of peripheral vision
- difficulty focusing on near or distant objects
- recurrent pain in or around eyes
- excess tearing or watery eyes
- dry eyes with itching or burning

The sun's rays damage our eyes all year long. Your parent will benefit from a good pair of UVA-protective sunglasses. Plastic lenses give up to 50 percent more protection from ultraviolet rays than glass.

Put light switches on the outside of rooms so your parent won't have to fumble for the switch in a dark room.

Modern technology now affords us "talking" clocks that announce the time, as well as talking thermometers, calculators, scales, computers, compasses, and even blood pressure devices. You can find them at seniorshops.com, among other places.

Remember that failing vision can come in many forms.

∽

"We didn't realize Dad was having a vision problem until he started showing up at our house in some of the weirdest outfits we'd ever seen—none of which ever matched. Even though he had no problem dressing himself, he was having trouble differentiating between colors. So I marked the colors of his shirts and trousers by writing the color onto the label with a laundry marker. Dad, who was always style conscious, was very appreciative."

—Susanne Colby

Cut out glare by using low-gloss wax on furniture and floors, avoiding fluorescent lights, and using sheer curtains on windows that offer plenty of sunlight. Walls should be painted with a matte finish.

Use contrasting colors in decorating, especially near thresholds and stairs. Paint banisters, doors, and thresholds in bright colors.

Wear contrasting colors when caring for someone with vision problems.

Keep small things such as the bottle opener, a nail file, a small set of scissors, and Dad's mustache trimmer on large key chains to make them easier to find. Or attach brightly colored ribbons and stickers that will make items like the TV remote, garden tools, and writing implements stand out.

Make sure that each chair in the house has a small reading lamp near it.

People with vision problems sometimes have trouble seeing white and clear objects. Clear drinking glasses, for instance, seem to disappear. Get tinted drinking glasses and brightly colored plates to avoid accidents.

You can buy a sheet of plastic (at seniorshops.com) that you place over a TV screen or computer to magnify the image.

If Grandpa's having vision problems but can still drive, help him find easier routes to his destinations. Driving on local streets (and avoiding rush hour traffic) instead of taking highways can make driving easier. Larger rear and side view mirrors make driving easier as well.

In ancient times, before TV, people actually sat around listening to the radio. Check out the wonderful programming offered by National

Public Radio, where you can still tune in to dramatic readings and tons of great programs that go far beyond "talk radio." Find programs your parent might enjoy, and remind him to tune in whenever the program is on.

Most insurance policies don't cover the cost of glasses and contact lenses, but Medigap does. Also Medicare Supplement Insurance picks up many costs that Medicare doesn't cover. Visit medicare.gov or contact your local Area Agency on Aging.

It's sometimes easier for a visually impaired person to watch a black-and-white TV instead of a color TV.

Soap operas are great for people who really can't focus on the TV but still want to follow stories. Visually, these programs rarely have much to offer anyway, and you miss little by just listening to an episode.

Audiobooks, or books on tape, are great when failing vision interferes with a love of reading. Most major releases are available on tape and CD these days. The library probably has a good selection, or you can even rent some great books and collections from recordedbooks.com. Make sure Dad knows how to use the tape or CD player and that spare batteries are kept handy.

Make generous use of magnifiers; they come in all shapes and sizes.

෴

"Mom constantly forgets where she's put the magnifier we got her. Now she wears a piece of jewelry that saves trouble and makes her the envy of her crowd: a lovely antique magnifying glass on a chain that I found at a flea market."

*—Randy Wysocki*

▶ Introduce your visually impaired senior to Talking Books, a free federally funded program that allows participants to borrow recorded books by mail. Call 1-202-707-5100 or go to loc.gov/nls for details.

▶ Hire a teen to come in the afternoon and read aloud to your parent. Local community groups also have reading volunteers.

▶ Go to concerts instead of movies.

▶ Increase lightbulb wattage around the house. Use three-way bulbs and dimmers for more flexibility.

▶ Around the house, make it a habit to put light objects on dark surfaces. If Mom can't see her brown comb on the mahogany dresser, get a colorful place mat for the dresser.

▶ Put fluorescent stickers and tape around light switches, keyholes, and doorknobs to make them easier to locate.

▶ Believe it or not, tight clothes can impair a person's vision by affecting the body's fluid system, including intraocular pressure, which leads to dry eyes. Does Grandma really need her girdle and pantyhose?

▶ If there's nothing to be done to improve vision and your mother's going to have to adjust to a new lifestyle, consult a low-vision specialist who can prescribe assistive devices. Contact the National Association for the Visually Handicapped (1-212-889-3141 or 1-415-221-3201) or Lighthouse International (1-800-829-0500 or lighthouse.org).

▶ When applying eyedrops, make sure you know which eye is being treated. Applying prescriptive drops to healthy eyes can be harmful.

If Mom likes to sew, find a tape measure with raised ridges that she can feel and a needle threader.

If your senior has failing vision, don't "help" him by cleaning up his house and reorganizing everything. Keep pathways clear, but otherwise learn to live with organized clutter if that's what he chooses.

You don't have to be elderly to have problems reading menus in restaurants. A small purse flashlight is useful for the purpose. Keep multiples handy.

People with vision problems have a much easier time with meals if they are served food of contrasting colors. Broiled fish served with rice and cauliflower can be a problem.

Playing cards with enlarged numbers can be found almost anywhere.

If your senior is visually impaired, announce yourself when you enter a room and say when you're leaving. Ask others to do the same, so your senior can keep track of who is in the room.

When walking together, let your loved one take your arm (rather than taking his), and ask him to follow your lead.

## INCONTINENCE

Learn about incontinence—its causes, its aids, and its widespread existence—so you can discuss it intelligently with your parent. If this isn't a conversation you are comfortable with, maybe another family member or a friend can help. In any case, be aware of Dad's feelings about it. Point out that these days, the adult diaper section in the supermarket is actually more extensive than the selection for babies. Tell him the size of the club he now belongs to: some thirteen million Americans suffer from various forms of incontinence. This isn't something that's happening just to him.

There are a number of treatments for incontinence. It should not be blindly accepted as part of the aging process. Your senior may have to learn to live with it (and there are many ways to do so comfortably), but before you accept that, consult with a physician about treatments—most often drugs and exercise, sometimes surgery. Many report success with biofeedback. Ask your doctor if it would make sense to refer your senior to a urologist.

Kegel exercises can help reduce incontinence. They're done by repeatedly tightening the muscles that control urinary flow, and they can be done while watching TV or pretty much anywhere. Ask your doctor for instructions, or go to depend.com/incont_educ_center/living_with_incont/kegel_exercises.asp.

Your senior should keep a log of fluid intake and bathroom visits. She might discover a pattern she can correct with some minor "bladder training," which involves holding it in for a short time to get herself onto a regular, convenient schedule.

Incontinence can be caused by nervousness and stress. Does your loved one have a problem she's not telling you about?

Maybe your father doesn't go to the bathroom as often as he needs to because he's afraid of falling. Is there a guard rail near the toilet? Is the toilet high enough? There are a variety of aids that will give him the security he might need.

Encourage a regular toilet routine. Set alarms to remind your senior to go to the bathroom, especially before bedtime.

Discourage Mom from using a sanitary pad instead of a diaper; it won't do the trick and will create more embarrassing problems, like odors. You can buy nondiaper underwear with built-in washable padding at medical supply houses.

Make sure the path to the bathroom is clear and easy to follow, with night-lights along the way. Is Grandpa's bedroom close enough to the bathroom?

If you have to question your parent about his bathroom habits, don't do so in front of others.

Have your mother dress in clothing that is quickly removed—no small buttons or snaps, please. Some clothing specially designed with incontinence in mind is available from Silvert's: 1-800-387-7088 (call for a catalog) or silverts.com.

When you and your senior visit someone's house or anywhere she hasn't been before, locate the bathroom on your arrival.

If your parents are no longer sleeping in the same bed because one of them is incontinent, get two single beds and move them next to one another.

If Grandma needs to spend a lot of time in the bathroom, make sure it's pleasant in there. Hang some pictures and have reading, photo albums, and/or music available.

Acidic foods such as tomatoes, oranges, pineapples, and grapefruit can irritate the bladder, as can smoking or even secondhand smoke.

Excess weight puts lots of extra pressure on the bladder.

Spray soiled clothing with stain remover and keep in a separate pail for soaking rather than adding the pieces to the other clothes in the laundry hamper.

Spray clothing with fabric protector right after it comes out of the dryer.

If laundering is taking up a good deal of your time, consider a laundry service that picks up and delivers. You've earned it!

Polyester and acrylic fabrics hold odors—cotton doesn't.

If you need to spray deodorizer in a room because your parent has had an accident, wait until she leaves the room.

Air-dry plastic sheets, or they will get brittle.

A wet washcloth dipped in baking soda gets rid of odors if applied right after an incident.

White wine vinegar eliminates the odor of urine almost immediately and works especially well on carpeting.

To clean feces from a person's body, use a tissue dabbed in petroleum jelly.

If you are helping your loved one with diapering, talk to him while you are doing it to put him at ease. Music can also make the procedure more pleasant.

Don't use talcum powder when you're changing a diaper; it attracts moisture and bacteria that can cause infection. A light application of a moisture barrier cream like petroleum jelly is best. Make sure any irritations you find are treated right away.

Get help. Visit incontinent.com for the latest treatments and devices that make living with incontinence easier.

Respect the dignity of your loved one. Ask permission before you work with private areas.

To clean feces off a floor, cover them with paper towels, pour some bleach over the towels (if carpeting is not a problem), and then gather it all up with clean paper towels. Place in a sealed bag for disposal.

Choose the odor fighter that works best for you:
- commercial deodorizer
- fan
- fresh air
- open box of baking soda
- squeezed lemon or orange in a bowl of water
- white vinegar

Look out for diaper rash and treat it promptly.

In restaurants, ask to be seated near the restroom.

Soiled diapers will be fine in an airtight container, but there are alternatives. Diaper Genies, which wrap and tightly compress used diapers, are hugely popular in baby care, and the wide-opening model by Playtex can accommodate adult diapers.

$\triangledown$ **7**

# Medical Treatment

ᏚᏒ

## DOCTORS

Find good doctors who specialize in geriatric care, which is one of the fastest-growing branches of medicine today. Your loved one may need to see one or more of the following kinds of doctors:

- cardiologist—heart and coronary artery specialist
- dermatologist—skin specialist
- endocrinologist—specialist in gland and hormone disorders
- gastroenterologist—stomach and digestive tract specialist
- gynecologist—specialist in the female reproductive system
- hematologist—blood specialist
- nephrologist—specialist in the function and diseases of the kidney
- oncologist—cancer and tumor specialist
- ophthalmologist—eye specialist who also performs eye surgery
- orthopedist—specialist in bone, muscle, and joint disorders
- otolaryngologist—ear, nose, and throat specialist
- proctologist—specialist of disorders of the anus, rectum, and colon

- pulmonary specialist—specialist in disorders of the lung and chest
- radiologist—x-ray specialist
- rehabilitation specialist—specialist in correcting stroke and injury disabilities
- rheumatologist—specialist in rheumatism and arthritis
- urologist—specialist in urinary systems in both sexes and in the male reproductive system

You can make yourself useful at the doctor's appointment by doing your homework before you go. Take just a little time to read up on your parent's condition. The doctor and your parent will both appreciate and respect your level of involvement, and the doctor will understand that your parent has a backup team that will be watching closely.

Having a team—including the doctor, other providers, you, other caregivers, *and your senior*—is a good general approach to take toward your senior's medical care. Encourage communication, cooperation, and respect among your teammates.

If there are lots of people in the family, appoint one person to deal with the doctor and then pass the information on to the others. Don't waste the doctor's time by asking her to repeat everything three times.

A doctor who refuses to include you in consultations and conversations when your parent wants you included is not the right doctor for you. Find another.

Be on the lookout for ageism, which has a tendency to occur among doctors who don't specialize in geriatrics. A doctor who tells a senior she can't be treated because her symptoms are due to "old age" and she should just get used to it may not know about the incredible advances that have recently been made in the field of gerontology—and has little respect for his patients, to boot. Look elsewhere for help.

Bring your senior's medical diary to every doctor's appointment. You can even take notes during the exam. For a complicated visit that you may want to share with others (or if you can't be there), can you arrange to tape the consultation? (Many doctors won't allow you to do this because of legal concerns, so inquire in advance.)

In your senior's medical diary, list the names of doctors you considered consulting but didn't. Note why you ruled them out.

All your parent's doctors need to be aware of one another. Keep them informed by faxing them copies of pages from your parent's medical diary.

If you use a group practice, your loved one will always have someone available to tend to him. But a single practitioner offers a more personal relationship. Generally, the elderly are better off in group practices, since their needs are often low on many doctors' priority lists.

Some fine specialists volunteer at clinics, and you can see them there for free.

If you are busy but want to accompany your loved one to a doctor's appointment, call the office and explain your schedule. Ask for an appointment during a time when you can be seen promptly. Confirm the appointment a number of times prior to showing up.

Just about every insurance program has a complicated referral system whereby you won't be reimbursed for expenses unless a general practitioner refers you to a specialist in writing prior to the appointment. Don't trust that these forms will get to the right desk. Ask that all referrals are faxed or sent to you, and then you will be the one to see that the form is sent to the proper office. (Make a photocopy and bring it with you to the appointment.) If that's not possible, call before the appointment to make sure the form from the referring physician has been received.

Don't assume that no news is good news. If your grandfather has taken a test and the results are overdue, follow up.

Ask Dad to introduce you to his doctor so that you will be familiar with one another if you need to communicate at any point. Let the doctor know how important your parent is to you and that even if you are not in the communication loop, you will always be there to watch out for your father.

Encourage your parent to talk to the doctor about personal developments as well as physical changes. Life changes can drastically affect anyone's health. Your doctor needs to see the big picture.

If you're going to have a lot of questions at the next appointment, or if you want to refer the doctor to an article you've seen, fax these to her a few days before the appointment. Don't ask her to go on the Internet to check something you're curious about. Send her a hard copy.

Make friends with the doctor's office manager. Let her know you appreciate her attention. Remember her at holiday time.

Before you take Grandma to a hospital or lab for a test, find out if the test can be done in a doctor's office.

If your parent adamantly refuses to see a doctor for what appears to be a minor condition, maybe you can get her to at least mention the problem to a pharmacist. Perhaps she'll take it more seriously if the pharmacist refers her to a doctor. You can also get free medical advice at medical fairs.

Find a doctor who is willing to conduct minor consultations over the phone.

The elderly may sometimes disrespect young doctors, whom they perceive as "Doogie Howsers." Apologize to the doctor privately and don't worry about it too much. He's probably heard it before.

If your father says or does things that are racist, sexist, or just plain rude to others, let him know directly that his behavior upsets you, and why. You can also apologize to the other person, but don't consider yourself responsible for your father's behavior. He is not your child and you're not raising him.

Some geriatricians make house calls. To find ones who do, contact the local Area Agency on Aging.

It's OK to switch doctors midstream if you're not pleased with your parent's care. Be sure to get copies of all records, which are your property.

Don't even think about attending a doctor's appointment without checking first to see if she's running on schedule. Senior patients are often the first to get bumped when there's a crunch.

Your father is likely to visit a variety of doctors for various problems, but one doctor—preferably the general practitioner or the internist he's been seeing the longest—should keep track of all the other doctors and what they're prescribing. When you make entries in your father's medical diary concerning a visit to a doctor, fax a copy to the main doctor and be sure to let her know what medications have been prescribed. Then call the office a day or two later and find out if she's reviewed your report. Should you be aware of any conflicts?

If your doctor's appointment depends on the results of tests that have been previously taken, check with the office before you leave for the appointment to make sure the results are in.

Even if you don't use Medicaid, know that Medicaid-approved physicians and medical facilities abide by the highest government standards.

At the doctor's office, don't answer questions for your parent unless you are asked to do so.

Having company on simple doctor visits can be reassuring and a nice outing. If you can, schedule something pleasant to do afterward.

Take a moment to memorize doctors' (and other important) phone numbers so you don't always have to look them up. This can be a real time-saver.

Make a list of questions and issues before you call the doctor. Take notes while he or she talks. Write these directly in your medical diary so you won't have to transfer them later.

Take your parent to the dentist. Ask if old fillings should be replaced. (Rotting teeth can cause havoc with one's hearing and balance, especially among seniors.)

Look into doctors practicing alternative medicine but be careful with natural medications—they can have serious side effects and/or interact with other medications.

Notify doctors and caregivers of alcohol and drug problems, even if you have to do it privately.

Be on the lookout for Medicare fraud, which hurts everyone. Check medical bills for waived fees and a wrong diagnosis on the claim form. If your doctor is using high-pressure tactics to entice your parent into a treatment you suspect he doesn't need, question it. Don't be shy about questioning anything you see on a doctor's bill. To report Medicare fraud, call 1-800-447-8477.

Make sure your loved one is comfortable with his doctor, that he feels good about openly discussing any and all problems. And make sure the doctor is one who takes the time to listen and provide complete explanations to all questions. If the doctor seems to prescribe the same medication time after time regardless of its effectiveness, switch doctors.

$\infty$

---

### Helpful Questions to Ask Your Senior's Doctor

- What—exactly—is the problem?
- Is my parent in any immediate danger?
- What are the short- and long-term effects?
- What medications will you prescribe and what are their side effects?
- What possible conflicts might there be in terms of treatment my parent is presently undergoing?
- What other treatments are possible?
- What will happen if the condition goes untreated?
- How much experience have you had with this particular problem?
- Will home assistance be necessary?
- What is the long-term prognosis?
- When should we expect to see a change? (How long should it take before the medication works?)
- When should we consult you next?
- Is there some way to prevent this in the future?

If there's a communication or language problem, make sure a translator is available for all doctor visits.

## MEDICATIONS

Invest in a copy of the *Physicians' Desk Reference (PDR)* or get information on medications online. Read up on each drug your loved one is taking, and feel free to ask questions when the *PDR* or website contradicts something the doctor may have said.

Check contraindications for all drugs.

Make sure that all doctors are aware of other medications and allergies before prescribing anything. If you keep a running account of meds, you can make copies and fax these regularly to the doctor.

Make friends with the local pharmacist and show your loyalty. Make him aware of your situation and your senior's general medical condition. He'll be a great source of information about new medications, discounts, and other remedies that can help your parent. And if all of your senior's prescriptions are filled there, he'll be able to keep track of them and spot a problem—like a bad interaction.

Ask the doctor for free prescription samples, especially when first trying out new medication.

Some medications really taste bad. Try different accompaniments until you find one that's least offensive. Some suggestions: chocolate pudding, applesauce, a teaspoon of honey or jam, Jell-O, cooked cereal, ice cream, and yogurt.

Higher concentrations of drugs (which you then cut in half with a pill cutter) save money.

It's not always OK to crush or dissolve certain pills before you take them; they may lose their effectiveness. Check with the pharmacist.

No matter how many times you pick up the same medication, always check to see that it's the correct one.

The hospital pharmacy is much more expensive than your local pharmacy. If you can, fill prescriptions from home.

If Mom keeps forgetting to take her medication, call her when it's time and ask her to take it while you're on the phone.

Some medications interact with sunlight; make sure you know if that's the case in your senior's situation.

It's often easier to swallow pills with water (or any liquid) sipped through a straw.

Most pharmacies will prepare large-print labels for prescription bottles if you ask for them.

♋

"Two of the sets of pills in my mother's medicine cabinet are about the same size, shape, and color. One is an allergy medication Mom usually only takes in the spring, and the other is to prevent heart failure. No one could figure out why her heart symptoms suddenly started to get worse and worse, until I happened to be right there when she went to take her meds. You can guess what I noticed—she was definitely allergy-free, but a couple more days of no heart medicine and she would have been in the emergency room. Now I put labels with LARGE print (medicine name, what it's for, and dosage directions) on all of the bottles, on top of the original ones."

—*Julia McCormack*

Constipation is a common side effect of many medications. If that's the case, consult the doctor about adjusting the dose or prescribing something in conjunction to alleviate the constipation.

Mark prescription refill dates on your calendar—at least a week before the present prescription runs out (or a month in advance if you get your prescriptions filled by a mail-order or online service).

If Dad subscribes to a free or low-cost mail-order drug program, he'll need two prescriptions: one to mail to the company and another to fill at a local pharmacy for an interim supply until the others are delivered.

Beware of online drug services that offer to send you prescription drugs without a prescription. You're likely to get expired drugs or pills without the actual medication in them.

Use a chalkboard or a dry erase board to keep track of medications on a daily basis. Put a check mark next to each pill when it's taken. The next morning, erase all the check marks and start all over again.

Remind Grandma to keep taking the prescription until it runs out and not to stop taking it just because she's feeling better.

When you are picking up a new prescription, it's a good idea to make sure the new pills look exactly like the old pills. If there's any difference, inquire.

Learn the names of the medications your parent is taking and what they do. The names are often confusing, but if you take a few minutes to memorize them, you'll save time later when you need to communicate with doctors and druggists.

Don't assume the generic equivalent of a drug is just as good as the brand-name version. Tell your pharmacist you want to be informed if your insurance company asks her to substitute generic drugs for whatever the doctor has prescribed. Call the doctor and ask if this is OK.

▶ Be sensitive to any alterations in your senior's condition that occur just after a medication or dosage has been changed.

▶ Make sure you know which meds need refrigeration. A lazy Susan— in the fridge or elsewhere—makes lots of little bottles accessible.

▶ You'll need to be especially patient while your mother is adjusting to new medication. This period can be frustrating, because until the dose that's just right for her is found, she'll continue to experience symptoms. "The drug isn't working" often means it hasn't been adjusted to work properly *yet*. Stay in touch with the prescribing physician, and let your parent know that relief is just around the corner.

▶ Use colored stickers to color-code medicine bottles so they can be identified easily.

▶ To help Mom remember to take a pill three times a day, put three rubber bands around the prescription bottle in the morning and have her remove a rubber band each time she takes the medication.

▶ One way for your senior to remember to take meds that aren't taken daily is to write the dosage on a calendar.

▶ If your loved one is taking an expensive maintenance drug, find out if he can save money by buying the drug in a ninety-day quantity and keeping it refrigerated.

▶ Does your mother's insurance company offer a special drug program that she didn't need until expensive medications were prescribed? Perhaps an update is in order.

When recording medications in your senior's medical diary, write down the name of the drug, the reason for taking it, the doctor who prescribed it, the dosage, and the dates of usage.

To find out whether your community has a drug assistance program for the elderly, as many do, contact the local Area Agency on Aging.

Don't keep medications in the bathroom, where moisture can affect them and they can easily be lost or flushed.

Ask the pharmacist to remind your parent when a prescription needs to be renewed.

With some medications, you can substitute a liquid for the pill version. Ask the pharmacist for more information.

If Mom keeps skipping her blood pressure medication, find out why. Does it make her nauseous? Is she shocked by how much it costs and forgetful of the fact that the insurance company is paying for it? Is she too tired to make trips to the pharmacy?

If there are no small children around, ask the pharmacist for easy-open bottles.

If medications consist of complicated combinations of pills, ask the pharmacist if she can put dosages in individual blister packs, each of which will contain all the pills to be taken at a time.

If your loved one is especially sensitive to his medications, make sure you're dispensing the proper amount of a liquid medicine by using a marked measuring spoon or a syringe that holds the exact dose (available at any pharmacy).

If your mother's fussy about taking her medication, don't make a big deal about it beforehand. Just announce that it's time to take the pill now and act like it's no big deal. (If you want to be sneaky, do this right before a favorite TV show or other pleasant activity. She'll be more eager to get the ordeal over with.)

▶ Know that most drugs are tested on middle-aged people, not the seniors who regularly take them. If there are any problems, don't hesitate to question the prescription.

▶ The idea is for your loved one to take as few drugs as possible. Question the doctor if it seems that she's prescribing an inordinate number of medications.

▶ Find out what time of day is best to take each drug. Some medications cause drowsiness; try to arrange for your loved one to take those in the evening.

▶ Clinical trials provide free drugs, but be aware that your senior may get a placebo. To find clinical trials that are overseen by the Food and Drug Administration (FDA), visit clinicaltrials.gov.

▶ Get rid of expired meds, not only because their effectiveness has been altered, but also because the clutter of extra bottles can result in Mom taking the wrong pill by mistake.

▶ If your parent is in a care facility, find out how much is being charged for prescriptions. It may be a lot cheaper for you to purchase these items independently.

∽

"The nursing home Dad was in must have been run by the same rocket scientists who sold the government $200 staplers and $800 toilet seats. We were being charged $4 for one aspirin! So I bought him his own bottle: I paid $4 for one hundred!"

—*Jonathan Buckles*

Missing even one dose of a medication can cause serious problems. When something goes wrong, ask if all medications have been taken.

Know what to do if a dosage is missed. It is *not* always better if Mom just takes the missed pills when you discover the mistake.

Keep medications in their original containers, especially if the containers are dark colored; many medications lose their effectiveness if left in the light. If you transfer pills to little dosage containers, keep the original bottles for reference.

Get day-by-day pill containers for medication.

If you are administering meds, tell Dad what you are giving him and what it will do for him.

Send for the free booklet *Free and Low Cost Prescription Drugs*, which lists hundreds of sources of free and discount medications. Published by the Cost Containment Research Institute in Washington, D.C., it lists opportunities by drug and by company. Even families with incomes of up to $50,000 are eligible. Send $5 to Institute Fulfillment Center, Prescription Drug Booklet #PDB-370, PO Box 210, Dallas, PA 18612-0210 or visit institutedc.org/edelivery.htm.

∾

"Check the pill containers often. I went to all this trouble to get Mom a pill organizer, since she took about sixteen pills a day, and Mom said it was all going well. Then my sister discovered that she was taking them day by day, all right, but she was taking all three doses in the morning 'in case I forget.' The answer was a twenty-four-hour timer, which we've set to go off when the meds are to be taken."

—*Pauline Twomey*

Clinical trials are conducted with new drugs that have been proven to have some benefits but which are not yet approved for public consumption. Alzheimer's disease is a common disease for which new approaches and cures are being constantly sought. But there are risks associated with clinical trials. Learn all the ramifications in a program before you decide to participate. To find out more about these procedures and which clinical trials are currently seeking participants, contact the National Institutes of Health (Bethesda, MD 20892) or visit clinicaltrials.com to browse through hundreds of requests for recruits.

# The Hospital

## Getting There

Keep a bag packed that is ready to accompany your loved one to every medical emergency, even if you don't think he will be admitted to the hospital. The bag should contain toothpaste, a toothbrush, a change of underwear, something to read or pass the time, pencil and paper, phone numbers, a snack, water or juice, towelettes, moisturizer, tissues, a favorite photo, a shaving kit, an extra pair of eyeglasses, a watch, health insurance information, and a copy of his medical diary. As he uses items from the bag, make notes to replace them.

If possible, don't take your senior to an emergency room (ER) until you know that her physician will be there prepared to admit her. The admitting doctor is the one who will be in charge of the case for the length of the hospital stay. Generally, triage nurses will put seniors at the bottom of the priority list, and as cruel as it may seem, leaving an elderly person in the ER for six to eight hours is not uncommon. If this is the case, be sure your senior has someone with her to keep her hydrated and as comfortable as possible.

There's no need to feel guilty if you chose a particular hospital just because it will make visiting more convenient for you. Your presence is liable to be the single most important element of your loved one's recuperation; knowing you're nearby can really make a difference.

As soon as Dad is admitted to the hospital, make contact with the discharge planner, who has some control over where he'll go after the hospital stay (if he can't go home) and what kind of care he'll get there. For this reason, you should start communicating (and maybe schmoozing a little) as soon as possible with this person whose decisions may have a major impact on your father's future. Starting a friendly dialogue may help ensure that Dad gets the posthospital care he needs.

Even if Mom is insured, ask if there's a private room available. If every bed is taken but the corner private room is sitting there empty, it's hers for the asking!

In the hospital, ask if there is a choice of rooms; go for the window side. There's less traffic and a better view.

When you arrive at the room your senior will occupy, call to arrange for TV and phone service immediately; it can take hours for these people to show up, and they often need to be paid in cash up front. Be sure to leave the receipt for the service with your parent in case there are questions. Also, find out what other services are available.

## In the Hospital

In a hospital, as in many large institutions, you're likely to encounter different opinions and conflicting advice from the various people involved in your senior's care. This can be very confusing and frustrating. If one doctor is prescribing diuretics for your father while another one wants to give him more fluids, try to get them into the same room so they can come to an agreement (and you and your senior can get off the seesaw they've created).

➤ If changes need to be made in your loved one's lifestyle, it may help to have an authority figure, such as a doctor, deliver the news, perhaps with you present.

➤ Don't get hysterical when your grandmother is put in the intensive care unit (ICU). It doesn't mean her condition is dire. Seniors are usually automatically admitted to the ICU.

➤ Protect the dignity of the patient. Ask permission before you work with private areas; ask people to leave the room; keep the curtains drawn even for a short procedure.

➤ Plastic bedpans are better than the metal kind, which get cold. If you use the metal kind, run warm water into it and around the rim. Dry thoroughly before it's used.

➤ Don't be intimidated by big words!

❦

"I was terrified at first and felt stupid when doctors and nurses threw terms at me that made my head spin. As the days went by, it seemed as if things were spinning out of control and I was agreeing to procedures I really didn't understand. When my sister flew in from Seattle, we went to the hospital together, and she gave me the courage to stand up to them and demand that they talk slower, explain terms, and provide all the information we needed to care for Mom."

—*Carly Novak*

If you need hired help, work with the doctor to determine what kind of help. A companion can stay with your parent but is not allowed to do much. If a medical situation arises, a companion is going to call a nurse for help. Nor will a companion be allowed to move your parent without a nurse assisting if there are mobility problems. A health aide can assist your parent more competently but cannot administer drugs. Even a nurse's aide (the next highest rung on the ladder) can only advise others of medical needs. Only a registered nurse can administer drugs and make substantive determinations about your parent's welfare. In any event, know that most hospitals are understaffed. If you want your parent to have close supervision and companionship, consider outside help.

When things get gross, reach for disposable gloves and breathe through your mouth.

Wash your hands often before, during, and after hospital visits, and wash your senior's hands just as often.

Bring a can of spray disinfectant to the hospital and spray it on doorknobs, telephone receivers, banisters, and so forth.

Post family phone numbers on large signs so Dad and the staff can see them easily, even if Dad can't use the phone. Post your own contact information boldly.

∽

"I can't believe how often I've heard 'We weren't able to contact you,' when the truth was, they were just too busy to look up my number in their files. Now my seventy-two-point computer-generated sign with my name and number leaves no room for excuses."

—*Derek Springer*

If your father can't eat on his own, ask the hospital's patient advocate if she can locate a volunteer who can help. Schedule your visits at mealtime so you can help out.

Find out what side effects are common with various procedures and warn your mother. Will her throat be a little sore after the gastroscopy? Withholding this kind of information will lead to distrust down the line, especially if she knows you knew and didn't tell her.

Get a telephone calling card (cell phones often don't work in hospitals).

Don't forget to suspend phone, mail, and delivery services while your senior is in the hospital. Notify his friends and social groups of his condition.

Hang up a sign with important information next to the patient's bed ("Patient is hard of hearing," "Patient not allowed sugar," etc.). If you're giving directives, always preface the instruction with "please."

Make sure Grandpa gets fresh air on a regular basis, even if that means sitting near an open window for twenty minutes a day.

Hospital gowns really do make sense. Don't be so quick to dress Mom in her cute pink nightgown if it's going to interfere with medical procedures and make her life more difficult. Does she really want to wear that pink nightgown or will it just make you feel better to see her in it? Get her a bed jacket (they still make them) to wear over the gown. Or bring a nice roomy kimono. Don't forget slippers with nonskid soles.

Try to get along with roommates, no matter how trying that may prove.

If you're at the hospital all day with your grandfather, put someone else in charge of communicating with other members of the family so you don't get home after a long day to seventeen phone messages.

If you've been caring for your parent at home, this hospital stay can be a respite for you. Take advantage of this "wiggle room." Hire teen sitters to stay at the hospital with your parent, even if it's just for companionship. Or call the local synagogue or church to find out if they can send a volunteer.

Pain management has become an advanced field all its own. Aside from medications, there are a number of other techniques (like breathing exercises, visualization) that work in many cases. If your senior is in pain, ask if there is a pain management specialist available for consultation at the hospital.

Ear plugs and a sleep mask in the hospital will help your mother to sleep.

Ask friends and family members to stagger visits so that your father's not inundated one day and lonely the next.

Tell the staff Mom's nickname. If everyone calls her Ella and she's now being addressed in the formal Gabriella, she might feel alienated. Post her name over her bed.

Don't ignore the parent who might be left at home. Does he need help around the house? Make it easy for him to get to the hospital for visits, and periodically give them some "alone" time together.

Don't let tubes and high-tech equipment keep you from making physical contact with your senior. He needs your love now more than ever, and even holding hands can make a huge difference.

Ask people with colds to stay away.

Don't bring large gifts to the hospital, even if it's Easter and that's the cutest six-foot bunny you've ever seen.

If there's a language problem, be present at important procedures to translate. If that's not possible, find out if you can "attend" the meeting via phone. You should also ask if the hospital has any translators available.

Before procedures, tell your loved one what to expect. If it's going to be uncomfortable, tell him for how long.

Hospital food can be pretty awful. Have a local restaurant deliver meals if that's possible. Bring tasty foods from home when you can. Suggest that visitors come at mealtime and bring prepared foods with them.

Keep a supply of paper plates and other disposables handy for snacks and foods you bring in from outside; it's easier and more sanitary.

If your senior is having major surgery and has never been in a hospital or in this particular hospital, bring her there a few days before just so she can get a feel for the place.

Make sure your parent follows all presurgery instructions.

Don't mistreat hospital staff. If you do, apologize after you have calmed down.

If you live far away from your parent, call the head nurse and develop a relationship with her. She'll be a great source of information. (When will the doctor most likely show up? What's the best way to get around visiting hours?) But don't squander her time.

Don't get annoyed if hospital staff members ask you to help care for your parent. They're not shirking their duties; they're just trying to involve you because they know how much it will help your parent to feel your presence.

Keep a running list of questions for the doctors, nurses, and other personnel. Leave a copy of this list with your parent and keep one for yourself.

Take advantage of the spiritual counseling available in the hospital, even if the counselor is of another faith.

☙

"Dad was rushed to St. Paul's Hospital when he had his heart attack; it was the nearest one to his office. We're Jewish, and frankly, I was put off, especially when Sister Sharon came by. I don't know if she was a nun, but I let her know I had no need to talk to her. She smiled and left a card with me that I was sure was some sort of Catholic prayer, and I tossed it aside. Later, as Dad's condition worsened, I found myself fussing around the room just to keep from crying. And I came across the card. I looked at it for the first time and was surprised to see a simple sentiment—the serenity prayer: 'God grant me the serenity to accept the things I cannot change, the courage to change the things I can, and the wisdom to know the difference.' What a comfort, and how good I felt knowing that Sister Sharon respected who I am and the difference between us. We wound up getting to know each other during the course of Dad's recovery; we learned about each other, and now I have a new friend."

—*Shoshana Baer*

Continuity in nursing care is extremely beneficial. If you are hiring private-care nurses, try to limit yourself to the same few, assuming your parent approves of these people. Find out who her favorites are.

Rehabilitation therapists tend to back off if your parent is resistant. If you think your parent just needs more time or encouragement, ask them to please keep trying. Support their effort by reminding your parent of all the good things that await her once she recovers.

## The Hospital Room Makeover

Luxuries from home can spruce up the place: scented soap, a lighted mirror, a special pillow (or even just a pillowcase), a throw, a framed photo.

Buy foam pillows or a "husband" pillow (the kind that supports the back and has armrests) for sitting up in bed.

Buy a bed desk.

It's not a good idea to wear or keep expensive items in the hospital. But if Mom's used to wearing jewelry and "feels naked" without it, substitute her valuables with some costume pieces for the time being. If they get lost or stolen, no big deal.

Make separate caddies (or use plastic bags or garden totes that have multiple compartments) for different activities: needlework, letter writing, reading, and so forth.

Bring a portable stereo with Dad's favorite and new music, audiobooks, and meditation tapes. Loved ones who can't visit can send recorded messages.

Use a room humidifier if the air is dry—vaporizers are better, being cheaper and more sanitary. In a pinch, a large bowl of water works, too—add a tiny bit of lemon, lime, or orange juice for a natural deodorizer.

It's really important to keep an eye out for bedsores and ask that any skin irritations be treated immediately. The head nurse will order a special foam "egg crate" mattress if you ask for one. Ask for one even if you don't think you need it.

Have games, coloring books, and other quiet diversions available for children if they are allowed to visit. Activities they can do both alone or with the patient are good choices. Checkers and ticktack-toe are games that most everyone enjoys.

A white noise machine can block out intercoms and other disturbing noises from the hallway.

See if a VCR is available for movies. Some hospitals have a video library.

Have "gum tack" available for putting up pictures, cards, and so forth. It won't hurt the walls, and you can take the stuff home when you leave.

Try to avoid having the TV on constantly.

As long as the hospital doesn't object, consider having a small aquarium or fishbowl in the room.

If there are visitors, try to have places for them to sit where they can be at eye level with the patient; avoid having a crowd looming over the bed.

Get a small refrigerator. There are tiny ones that hold as little as four cans of soda.

A stuffed animal (especially if it's a gift from someone special, like a child) can be a comfort.

## Going Home

When it comes to rehabilitation, remember that hospital personnel probably never met your parent until he entered the hospital, and they can't know what his true baseline is. Attend the meetings at which your parent is being discussed, and make sure their goals are the same as yours. But be realistic about expectations. Your parent's baseline will probably change as a result of a hospital stay, especially if surgery is necessary.

If Mom has been out of the home for some time, even if Dad has been maintaining the home, consider hiring a cleaning service to come the day before Mom comes home to make sure everything is clean and fresh.

When you leave the hospital and are given follow-up information, make copies for other caregivers and family members.

When you leave the hospital, be sure to add copies of all written instructions and follow-up procedures to your senior's medical diary.

Have hospital staff demonstrate techniques for diapering and for assisting with walking, standing up and sitting down, feeding, bathing, and so on. Consider the hospital stay a learning experience, and take advantage of the fine teachers you have at your (free) disposal.

If a nurse or other caregiver will take care of your parent after a hospital stay, have that person meet you at the hospital when your parent is discharged. Give the caregiver a chance to observe the way in which you relate to your parent.

Make sure all tests and procedures are *really* necessary. Can any of them be done on an outpatient basis?

〜

## The Patient's Bill of Rights

These rights can be exercised on the patient's behalf by a designated surrogate or proxy decision maker if the patient lacks decision-making capacity, is legally incompetent, or is a minor.

1. The patient has the right to considerate and respectful care.
2. The patient has the right to and is encouraged to obtain from physicians and other direct caregivers relevant, current, and understandable information concerning diagnosis, treatment, and prognosis.
3. Except in emergencies when the patient lacks decision-making capacity and the need for treatment is urgent, the patient is entitled to the opportunity to discuss and request information related to the specific procedures and/or treatments, the risks involved, the possible length of recuperation, and the medically reasonable alternatives and their accompanying risks and benefits.
4. Patients have the right to know the identity of physicians, nurses, and others involved in their care, as well as when those involved are students, residents, or other trainees. The patient also has the right to know the immediate and long-term financial implications of treatment choices, insofar as they are known.
5. The patient has the right to make decisions about the plan of care prior to and during the course of treatment and to refuse a recommended treatment or plan of care to the extent permitted

by law and hospital policy and to be informed of the medical consequences of this action. In case of such refusal, the patient is entitled to other appropriate care and services that the hospital provides or transfer to another hospital. The hospital should notify patients of any policy that might affect patient choice within the institution.

6. The patient has the right to have an advance directive (such as a living will, health care proxy, or durable power of attorney for health care) concerning treatment or designating a surrogate decision maker with the expectation that the hospital will honor the intent of that directive to the extent permitted by law and hospital policy.

7. Health care institutions must advise patients of their rights under state law and hospital policy to make informed medical choices, ask if the patient has an advance directive, and include that information in patient records. The patient has the right to timely information about hospital policy that may limit its ability to implement fully a legally valid advance directive.

8. The patient has the right to every consideration of privacy. Case discussion, consultation, examination, and treatment should be conducted so as to protect each patient's privacy.

9. The patient has the right to expect that all communications and records pertaining to his or her care will be treated as confidential by the hospital, except in cases such as suspected abuse and public health hazards when reporting is permitted or required by law. The patient has the right to expect that the hospital will emphasize the confidentiality of this information when it releases it to any other parties entitled to review information in these records.

10. The patient has the right to review the records pertaining to his or her medical care and to have the information explained or interpreted as necessary, except when restricted by law.

11. The patient has the right to expect that, within its capacity and policies, a hospital will make reasonable response to the request

of a patient for appropriate and medically indicated care and services. The hospital must provide evaluation, service, and/or referral as indicated by the urgency of the case. When medically appropriate and legally permissible, or when a patient has so requested, a patient may be transferred to another facility. The institution to which the patient is to be transferred must first have accepted the patient for transfer. The patient must also have the benefit of complete information and explanation concerning the need for, risks, benefits, and alternatives to such a transfer.

12. The patient has the right to ask and be informed of the existence of business relationships among the hospital, educational institutions, other health care providers, or payers that may influence the patient's treatment and care.

13. The patient has the right to consent to or decline to participate in proposed research studies or human experimentation affecting care and treatment or requiring direct patient involvement, and to have those studies fully explained prior to consent. A patient who declines to participate in research or experimentation is entitled to the most effective care that the hospital can otherwise provide.

14. The patient has the right to expect reasonable continuity of care when appropriate and to be informed by physicians and other caregivers of available and realistic patient care options when hospital care is no longer appropriate.

15. The patient has the right to be informed of hospital policies and practices that relate to patient care, treatment, and responsibilities. The patient has the right to be informed of available resources for resolving disputes, grievances, and conflicts, such as ethics committees, patient representatives, or other mechanisms available in the institution. The patient has the right to be informed of the hospital's charges for services and available payment methods.

# PART III

# PEOPLE WHO NEED PEOPLE

∽

# Staying Close

∾

## COMMUNICATING, CONNECTING, AND COPING

▸Your ability to communicate well with your senior, to understand him as well as be understood, is possibly the most important factor in your experience as a caregiver. If you've never communicated very well, that means there is plenty of room for improvement!

▸In communicating with your senior, make it your goal to continually practice respect and patience. Periodically put yourself in her position and ask yourself how you would want to be spoken to and heard.

▸Call at the same time every day for the purpose of contributing to a regular routine. But occasionally call at odd times, too, just so your conversations don't become boring and predictable for both of you.

▸Most answering services provide wake-up calls and other daily reminders. The friendliest of these will even routinely check on your loved one. To find such providers look under "Telephone Answering

Services" in the Yellow Pages. But don't substitute phone services for the love and security that only a family member can provide.

Avoid missing Dad or interrupting a favorite activity when you call by keeping a copy of his schedule next to your own.

Don't repeatedly cancel visits. Just as the dashed hopes of a child can be perceived as tragedy, so might a cancelled visit, especially when it has been eagerly anticipated. If your schedule needs to remain flexible, let your senior know. Don't set dates and times for visits until you're sure you can follow through. You'll protect your loved one from disappointment and keep yourself from feeling guilty.

Get to know and develop a relationship with your senior's best friends, even if you're not crazy about them. Recognize how important their support is, or may be in the future, to your loved one, especially if you can't be around yourself.

Befriend Mom's mail carrier, neighbors, and shop owners so that they are aware of your loved one. These people can be a valuable source of information regarding anything unusual in her behavior.

෬⌇

"We always visit my mother-in-law around the holidays, especially now that she's alone. While I'm there I've started giving cash gifts to the mailman, the trash collectors, the landscapers, newspaper deliverer . . . all the people you'd normally recognize during the holidays, along with a note from the whole family thanking them for their good service. She doesn't think to take care of it, and she's on a fixed income. I'm making sure they get taken care of so that they'll take good care of her."

—*Danny Weinberg*

∽

## Fifty Great Gifts for Seniors

1. air purifier
2. aromatherapy candles and sprays
3. audiobooks and a portable listening device
4. autographed photo of a favorite actor or sports star
5. bed jacket or shawl
6. blank journal
7. bulletin board
8. calendar
9. cell phone
10. change purse filled with transportation tokens
11. collage of family photos
12. copy of a newspaper from a special date
13. exercise mat or light weights
14. eyeglass chain
15. family portrait
16. footrest or foot massager
17. fresh or silk flowers
18. gift certificate for a manicure or pedicure
19. hat
20. home cleaning service
21. home maintenance service
22. "husband" pillow
23. large-type books
24. lightweight dishes
25. lightweight pots and pans
26. limousine company services
27. loofah and bath products
28. magazine subscriptions
29. magnifying mirror
30. moisturizer
31. old "home movies" converted to VHS
32. pedometer
33. photo album
34. picture book about a favorite place or activity
35. picture frame
36. plants
37. portable telephone
38. prepaid phone card
39. prepared foods
40. quilt
41. reflective clothing
42. restored version of an old, damaged photo
43. scarf
44. shopping cart
45. star named after them
46. stationery with postage included
47. stuffed animal
48. videotapes of great films
49. water filter
50. white noise machine

▶ Is there someone in your community who may not get around easily but who would make a great phone pal for Mom? A great new friendship might ensue.

▶ If you live far away, ask the telephone company for a copy of the Yellow Pages covering your parents' community so you can help locate resources when you need them.

▶ If you or other family members live far away, post a list of time zone equivalents (in your home and theirs) to make staying in touch easier.

▶ Hire a local home maintenance service on a seasonal basis. A fall "package," for instance, might include heating unit filter changes, hot water tank maintenance, smoke detector battery replacement, dryer vent cleaning, window screen replacement, and exterior light timer adjustment. What a great idea for a gift!

▶ Talk to your senior about the relationships she has had with the older people in *her* life. Did Mom ever need to take care of her parents? What does she remember about it, both bad *and* good? What did she learn?

▶ Emphasize your shared experience as much as possible.

෴

"After Dad died, I was really worried about Mom's ability to deal with their finances. I let her know that I was (truthfully) concerned about what would happen if my own husband were to pass away, since he handles most of our money issues. That opened up the discussion to her situation, and we decided that both of us should talk to a financial adviser."

—*Ronnie Paliscano*

➤ Organize siblings and other family members into a "telephone tag team." You each take turns calling to make sure your parents are OK, and you use chain calling to keep the others informed. If there are enough people on the team, your parents can get at least one call each day, and maybe more. Similarly, get the little ones in the family to send letters, cards, and drawings. They, too, can take turns so that Mom and Dad get something fun in the mail almost every day.

➤ Whenever possible, seek out your loved one's opinion and wishes when making a decision. Don't assume that you know what she wants, how she feels, or what she's thinking. Ask her.

➤ Apologize when you make a mistake. (You will find this easier to do when you accept that you are human and cannot do everything perfectly. For more on this, see Chapter 10, "Taking Care of You.")

➤ Don't assume Dad is OK just because he says he is. Keep your eyes and ears open, and keep volunteering to help no matter how often he turns you down. Your continued offers will at least remind him that help is always there when he's ready to ask for it.

〰

"My father feels so guilty and embarrassed for all (as he puts it) the trouble he puts us through. He is constantly apologizing and making a big deal out of every little thing we do for him, even though I try to downplay and make light of it as much as possible. When he starts to get on a roll, I stop him by reminding him of some of the things that he did for me when I was growing up, like the dollhouse he built for me or when he risked life and limb teaching me to drive (even after I dented the car). I let him know how important it is to me—how good it makes me feel—to return the favor."

—*Pat D. Bruno*

Encourage an atmosphere of teamwork when discussing problems, even disagreements. "You seem upset with me for not calling as often as you'd like, and I'm unhappy because I just can't give you more attention because of my other obligations. How can we figure out a way for both of us to feel better about this?"

The less you see your father, the more pronounced his deterioration is likely to appear when you see him again. When you are a long-distance caregiver, try to stay on top of physical (or other) changes by asking other family members who live closer to keep you informed. Try not to look shocked when you see Dad.

Raise sensitive issues by talking about them indirectly. If you're worried about your mother's health, start by talking about your concerns over a friend's serious illness (or better yet, does she have a friend whom she's concerned about?).

Even long distance, Grandma and your young one can color together. Buy a coloring book and two boxes of crayons. Send the coloring book to Grandma after your child has colored part of a picture and ask her to do the rest. Then she starts a picture and your child finishes it. Chain stories are fun to write, in much the same way.

It's a fact of life that not only are being right and being happy two different things—they're often mutually exclusive. For the sake of everyone, pick your battles and know when to lose an argument.

Have rules about how arguments will be settled.

※

"There's no rhyme or reason to our bickering. I think Mom and I do this all day long because it's something to do. No one even cares anymore who wins. So we just take turns being 'right.'"

—*Marcia Juan*

▶ Don't inundate your senior with lots of information at one time. Remember that it often takes seniors a few moments to "switch gears" (i.e., change subjects).

▶ Tell jokes. Just don't be too surprised to hear that the hilarious one your coworker sent to you by E-mail is almost as funny today as it was in 1947.

▶ Ask specific questions, not general ones: "Would you like soup or a sandwich?" is better than "What do you want to eat?" After you ask a question, give Grandma plenty of time to answer.

▶ Positives are better than negatives when communicating: "Let's talk about your birthday" is better than "Let's not argue."

▶ Respect cultural differences. Approach your senior as you would an honored guest who was raised in a land very different from your own. Perhaps this is the case, but even if it isn't, he was raised in a different time, and therefore in a different world.

▶ If your senior has speech problems, keep a pad of paper and a pen handy at all times, or get her a small dry erase board for messages.

▶ Accept limitations. It may be hard to face that your loved one can't do things the way he used to, but change is inevitable.

⚬⚬

"Dad was always such a wonderful pianist, and it was awful when he had the stroke and couldn't play anymore. When he recovered somewhat, my brother and I started pushing him to try playing again, but he just couldn't. I realized I had to let it go. Now we go to concerts together or listen to recordings, and he always gives me his expert critique afterward."

—*Hillel Wein*

▸Don't choose this time to unburden yourself. Knowing that your father is nearing the end of his life or being in the position of caring for him may tempt you to confront him about his criticisms of you when you were a child or the feeling that he seemed to prefer your brother over you. If you haven't resolved an old issue with him directly before, at this point you'll most likely just upset him without getting a satisfactory response that will help you feel better. Work through it with a counselor or a good friend, and move on.

▸A speech pathologist can help keep the lines of communication open. If your senior has a speech problem, consult a professional before you accept the condition. It may be caused by medication or some other treatable problem.

▸If you feel like you're always quizzing your senior, try turning some questions into answers: "There's the bathroom" is better than "Do you have to go to the bathroom?"

▸Don't finish a senior's sentences. It's rude, and unless you're a mind reader, you really don't know what he's going to say next.

▸Ask your senior for advice.

ᴏⱱᴏ

"I've started doing a lot of things for my father over the past couple of years as his health has gotten worse, and he appreciates it, but I know it makes him uncomfortable to be dependent on me. I noticed that if I talk to him about some of my problems, like the difficult client I was dealing with last month, it makes him feel like the relationship is more give-and-take. Plus his advice works!"

—*Jerry Hamerick*

▶ Cut out pictures of everyday objects from magazines, and paste these onto index cards for a speech-impaired senior. Have him point to the cards to help him communicate.

▶ Technology has come a long way in assisting the vocally impaired to communicate. Talking software allows people to use computers or portable devices such as a communication board to converse with others in person and over the telephone. You can search Abledata, a database for products that might meet your senior's needs, at abledata.com.

▶ Recognize that certain conversations may need several "installments."

▶ Don't have a solution for everything. Sometimes Mom may just need you to listen. Respect her right to whine.

▶ Touch is an underrated form of communication. Often when words fail, it helps just to hold each other.

▶ Bad news about others can sometimes be a useful distraction.

ᕙᕗ

"For the longest time, we kept bad news from my mother, figuring she'd worry herself to death if we shared all the trials and tribulations that families normally go through. Then one day, someone accidentally spilled the beans about her nephew having had a heart attack. But instead of taking the news hard, Mom showed concern and caring, and the ordeal actually took her mind off her own troubles for a few days. Looking back on it, I think what perked her up was the reminder that she's still a strong, vital part of our family and that her support is still important to us all."

—*Kate Bechtold*

When you feel frustrated, count to ten. If that doesn't work, count to one hundred. If that doesn't work, keep counting.

Nobody likes a know-it-all. Remember, your senior is a firsthand expert on getting older, and you aren't (no matter how many books you read).

Respect old habits. Indeed, they die hard. You may know a faster route to the post office or a more efficient way to organize the bills, but if Grandpa can still do it OK on his own, try to let him be.

In a near crisis or often a real crisis, there will be time enough to deal with the worst if and when it comes to fruition. In the meantime, you'll think more clearly if you stay focused on what is going on at the present moment.

Ask yourself what you will be like when you are old. How will you feel in similar situations? How will you react to the things your parents are experiencing right now?

Don't take combative behavior personally. More likely than not, you're just the nearest or only available person on which your senior can release frustration.

$$\curlyvee$$

"We've never been a Norman Rockwell family, and when the situation gets tough, we end up using the same dark, sarcastic humor as always. I threaten to lock Mom in the closet 'again' if she doesn't take her medicine; she swears that the cat will be the sole beneficiary in her will if I don't stop nagging her. Obviously none of it's true, but the more outrageous we make it, the more it cuts through the very real tension we're feeling. In a way it puts it into perspective, too."

—Tansey Marsh

Let your mother make choices when possible: which color to wear, how to decorate a room, which food to eat first.

Give your senior jobs to do. Ask him for small favors. Keep the help going in both directions.

If Dad just won't stop ranting about how things have changed and how "they don't make them like that anymore," help him tell it to someone who cares—the president of the United States! To give the White House a piece of your mind, call 1-202-456-1111. We're not guaranteeing results, but the experience can be very empowering!

The human body, even older models, can bounce back from myriad difficulties. Here, more than anywhere else, *you never know.*

Avoid saying "everything happens for a reason." Some people, particularly survivors of wars and disasters, have had to endure unimaginable ordeals that one can never make sense of. Saying "everything happens for a reason" to such a person makes him wonder if he may have brought those nightmares on himself.

Laugh together—even at the most embarrassing moments.

Make up rhymes, sayings, and rituals that you say together in times of stress.

෧෨

---

"When we were little, Dad used to have this funny thing he did: whenever something went wrong, he'd say, 'I guess my guardian angel screwed up big this time around!' Now, when things go badly, I blame it on Dad's guardian angel, and it always gets a smile out of him."
—*Julius Paterson*

Talk about the miracles of modern medicine and the progress we have made this last generation.

Don't ignore the spiritual needs of your senior, even if those needs are different from your own. Help Mom attend religious services if she has the desire and ability. If she is housebound, almost all religious communities offer home visits.

Don't make a big deal about new additions to the picture, like a wheelchair or the need to use diapers. Introduce these things as a matter of course, and let your loved one express his feelings about it. Don't tell him how to feel about these life changes.

When Mom fusses no matter what you do for her and it seems as though nothing can make her happy, even for the moment, ask yourself whether the solution might be something much simpler. Think about what children like. They like to feel good. What feels good? A hug, a song, or something pretty to look at. Don't overlook the little things; they can make a big difference.

Set short- *and* long-term goals. Make New Year's resolutions together. Count on the future.

Make a small tape recorder part of your arsenal of lifesavers, and make sure your father knows how to use it. Music and audiobooks can be endlessly entertaining, and when friends can't visit, you can bring a taped message. And be sure to encourage Dad to record his life story for posterity—a real treasure for future generations.

## Could You Just Listen?

People who cannot express themselves yearn to be heard. Here are some lessons in listening that seniors would like to teach us:

- When I ask you to listen to me and you start giving me advice, you have not done what I asked.
- When I ask you to listen to me and you begin to tell me why I shouldn't feel that way, you are trampling on my feelings.
- When I ask you to listen to me and you feel you have to do something to solve my problem, you have failed me, strange as that may seem.
- Listen! All I asked was that you listen, not talk or do—just hear me.
- Advice is cheap—spare change will get you both Dear Abby and Billy Graham in the same paper.
- When you do something for me that I can and need to do for myself, you contribute to my fear and feelings of inadequacy.
- When you accept as a simple fact that I do feel what I feel, no matter how irrational, then I can quit trying to convince you and can get about this business of understanding what's behind this irrational feeling. When that's clear, the answers will be obvious and I won't need advice.
- Please listen, and just hear me.

## STAYING CONNECTED

Senior Corps, through the Corporation for National and Community Service, runs three programs: the Foster Grandparent Program (seniors help abused kids), the Senior Companion Program (volunteers help seniors with day-to-day tasks), and the Retired and Senior Volunteer Program (seniors use their life experience to help others). All programs are flexible; any can change a life. Call 1-800-424-8867 or visit seniorcorps.org.

Check out aarp.com/volunteerguide for ideas, resources, and advice for potential senior volunteers. Some possibilities include libraries, museums, local schools, and day care centers.

Elderhostel (1-877-426-8056 or elderhostel.org) offers year-round programs for seniors at colleges around the world.

Seniors can share their knowledge with others over the Internet and get paid for it! At lifetips.com (or call 1-617-886-9001, extension 201), seniors are invited to become gurus in various subjects. The website provides all the instructions, and the guru gets a share of the income generated by his or her advice.

The National Gallery of Art has videos and slide programs available to individuals and groups. All you have to do is pay the postage both ways. For a catalog of what's available, write to the National Gallery of Art, Extension Program, Washington, DC 20565 or visit nga.gov.

The TV networks give away free tickets to shows that have live audiences—an interesting, inexpensive outing.

SCORE big: the Service Corps of Retired Executives, working with the U.S. Small Business Administration, offers ways for people to come together with seasoned experts for everyone's benefit. Call 1-800-634-0245 or visit score.org.

Volunteering is an especially good way to remind seniors that they are still vital, important members of the community. Find associations and services that need help. Try to match your parent's talent or ability with a particular need.

෴

"Mom was always a great seamstress and missed her sewing once she gave up the business. Now she's wardrobe mistress at our local drama society and loves it."

*—Virginia Lowell*

▸Send your senior to summer school! Several college campuses in the United States and Canada offer sessions that last from two to ten weeks. No grade, no mandatory attendance—just lots of real learning and new experiences. Contact Senior Summer School, PO Box 4424, Deerfield Beach, FL 33442-4424, 1-800-847-2466, or E-mail seniorsummerschool.com.

▸Check with your local community center and/or library to see what kinds of programs they offer. They will often have classes, lectures, and book clubs and serve as meeting places for various organizations and clubs. Clubs that seniors may enjoy run the gamut from quilting, card playing, gardening, and any other type of activity or hobby. Find one that might interest your father, and again, go along as well until he makes a few friends and feels comfortable going alone. Don't forget to check your local paper for an events calendar in your area, too.

▸Even if your parent doesn't want to enter the Seniors Softball World Series, he may want to be a spectator. Find out more about senior athletic competitions by contacting your local senior center or the U.S. National Senior Games Association, PO Box 82059, Baton Rouge, LA 70884, 1-225-766-6800, nsga.com.

▸Encourage your senior to take an adult education course, even if it's a subject in which she had no prior interest.

ᘐᕘ

"As it turned out, Aunt May discovered more about herself in her senior years than she did in all the years she worked as a career counselor. She took a course in basic photography at the local community center only because it was the only course given at a time when she could easily attend. Now it's her new passion."

—*Rachel Hitner*

▶ Start a community garden and get other seniors involved. If there's no public plot of land for you to use, maybe you can get permission from home owners and apartment building landlords to landscape their property. For teaching tools and information on community gardening, write to the National Gardening Association, 1100 Dorset Street, South Burlington, VT 05403 or visit garden.org.

▶ Create an abbreviated TV listing by downloading the information off tvguide.com and deleting all the channels you know Mom doesn't care about. It'll be easier for her to locate her favorite programs on a shorter listing. Or go through her TV listing and highlight the shows you think she'll like.

▶ Would your loved one enjoy receiving a special message from the president of the United States? If your parents are celebrating their fiftieth (or beyond) anniversary or if either of them is eighty or older, send your request at least four weeks in advance to The Greetings Office, The White House, Washington, DC 20500, or fax your request: 1-202-395-1232. You can have the letter sent to yourself and get it framed in time for a special day.

▶ If your senior is healthy, able, and looking for some company and diversion while making money, perhaps she should consider pet sitting.

⟨୨⟩

---

"My mother has become the 'doggie grandma' on her block. Two of her neighbors work all day, so they leave their (well-behaved) pooches with her in the morning. She plays with them in the backyard for a while; then they lie on the floor while she watches her soaps. The owners feel less guilty that the dogs aren't alone all day, and Mom gets some extra cash and the companionship, without the responsibility of owning a pet herself."

—Sara Dileo

▶ Gardening is a wonderful hobby for almost anyone, as it can be done in a form so simple as planting a seed in a small container and watching it sprout to installing a full-scale vegetable garden that is also a food source. Check out garden clubs.

▶ Get large-type books and magazines. Many magazines offer large-print editions, which are available at most libraries. If they're not, request that they be stocked.

▶ If Dad is a sports enthusiast, he might like to have an autographed photo of his favorite player. Most sports teams offer these—and other freebies—to loyal fans who write and ask for them.

▶ Crooked cards that come in odd shapes (sort of zigzagged on the sides) might enable your grandfather to play bridge despite the trouble he may have gripping things.

▶ If your senior can't attend an important family event, perhaps you can arrange a less elaborate version of the festivities in a more accessible setting.

ॐ

"Lara was devastated when we learned, the day before her wedding, that her beloved grandmother would not be able to attend the event. We went through with the service and reception, but the next day, about ten of us—including Lara and Eldar in full wedding-day regalia—went over to the nursing home and reenacted the event. Our rabbi presided over an informal version of the original ceremony, and all the residents attended and shared cake. We were later told that it was one of the most exciting events that had ever taken place at the home and that other families were now being encouraged to share festivities with those who might otherwise be left behind."

—*Shirley Samelson*

▶ Audiobooks are available at libraries and are wonderful when eyesight and concentration fail. Also look for an "audiotape exchange" in the Yellow Pages. These businesses allow you to trade your used audiobooks for others.

▶ Nurture friendships.

▶ "Translate" an old hobby (needlepoint) that can no longer be managed into something more simple but similar (gros point). If Dad was a bridge player, he might like a simple game of rummy or even war, just to be playing cards again. Make up card games and remember that every game does not have to have a winner and a loser. If Mom can't knit anymore, check out knitting machines.

▶ Help your loved one mark the passage of time. Talk about the season, the month, and upcoming holidays and events. Remind her always that there is a future.

▶ Give your parent jobs to do. Everyone needs a daily purpose.

ᘐᗞ

"The worst thing about Mom's stroke was the fact that she finally had to give up her addiction to work. She seemed so lost until my twelve-year-old, who was running for school president, tried to enlist my help stuffing about 650 envelopes with campaign flyers. It gave me an idea: I told Joey I didn't have time to help but that if he rode his bike over to his grandma's, he'd have a willing, enthusiastic volunteer. She was thrilled to help. Since then we have found small jobs that Mom can handle: sorting the coupons I clip each week, rolling spare change, helping the kids out with their craft projects, and so on. Sure, these things would be easy for me to do in a flash, but Mom loves these jobs, and they make her feel useful."

—*Rachel Gotsch*

▸ Some volunteer work (e.g., stuffing envelopes, making phone calls) can be done from home.

▸ Bring kids to visit; even kids your mother doesn't know are fun to have around. (Do any of your neighbors need some time alone?)

▸ If your loved one has a talent for crafts, and you think her creations might sell well at fairs, find out more about marketing these creations by writing to Elder Craftsmen, 921 Madison Avenue, New York, NY 10012.

▸ Did Mom or Dad serve in the military? Find out about reunions or help them contact old comrades at va.gov.

▸ Teach each other something new. Maybe Mom taught you how to make cookies or to ride a bike, but you never learned embroidery or how to speak the language from "the old country." In the meantime, you can teach her something from your own bag of tricks.

▸ Encourage romance. If this offends you in some way, get over it.

▸ Throw small parties for your parent's friends.

⌒◦

"After Mom passed away, Dad was lonely for his friends but didn't have a clue as to how to entertain them the way Mom had, and he didn't feel right inviting people over just for coffee. So I started throwing small parties for his friends—sometimes at my house, often at his apartment—and this really helped him stay in touch and in the swing of things. I'm sure this has a lot to do with the great shape he's in today."

—*Meryl Salavant*

Don't bring old friends to visit who may do little else but mourn the past. Keep visits as upbeat as possible. That doesn't mean you should deny the past, only that you might not want to dwell on it.

Look into computer education courses at the local college, the library, the YMCA, or even a local senior center. Some places have classes designed just for seniors.

At the risk of offending Bill Gates, an Apple iMac is a great choice for seniors. It's very easy to use and comes with clear directions, unlike Windows. Your father doesn't need to worry about his computer being compatible with the one at work or about getting all the latest software anyway.

Valentine's Day is a great occasion to demonstrate your love for the seniors in your life. Send them valentines and get them involved with any celebrations you might plan. Don't forget that anyone who has lost a spouse is especially fragile around Valentine's Day.

Learn and teach Grandma a prayer. You can request a free copy of the King James version of the Bible from The Church of Jesus Christ of Latter-Day Saints by calling 1-800-535-1118. You will be asked if you would like to speak with a church member, but it's OK to decline.

The Internet is a door to the world. Set your senior up with an Internet provider and encourage her to get online.

∽

"My grandmother enjoys visiting museum websites and using the Internet to keep in touch with her grandchildren. Last year she started searching for some of her long-lost relatives and managed to surf her way into a family reunion in Barcelona!"

—*Michael Palmer*

If your senior can't attend a family event because it's going to go on long after his bedtime, arrange for him to at least attend part of the event. Hire a companion who can escort him home when it becomes necessary. Even if he's able to stay for the whole event, a companion will ensure that he has constant attention. You don't have to announce that he's with a paid companion. If he's embarrassed, introduce the person as a family friend, and ask the companion to dress appropriately for the occasion.

Ask Grandpa to join you in a new hobby. Learn something new together.

Keep your senior updated on current events. Read the newspaper or watch or listen to the news together *and talk about the events.*

Read aloud. You might try a new book that would interest you both, or read an old favorite.

Share your work with Dad. Let him know about the new project you're working on or what's brewing in office politics. Just adjust the complexity to fit his understanding.

Be sad together. You don't always have to try to cheer up Mom right away—maybe a good cry together is what you both need.

Be patient and remember that your senior's generation did not grow up having computers or using them at work.

෨෨

"I've had to go over to my grandmother's many times when she's told me it's 'broken,' only to find out that she's somehow covered up her entire desktop with 'untitled folders.'"

—*Shannon Michaels*

▶Watch movies together. Talk about them.

᠁

### Ten Classic Comedies

1. *Bringing Up Baby*
2. *It Happened One Night*
3. *The Philadelphia Story*
4. *The Thin Man* (series)
5. *The Miracle of Morgan's Creek*
6. *The Lady Eve*
7. *Some Like It Hot*
8. *Adam's Rib*
9. *Born Yesterday*
10. *Ninotchka*

### Ten "New Classic" Comedies

1. *Groundhog Day*
2. *When Harry Met Sally*
3. *Young Frankenstein*
4. *Annie Hall*
5. *Tootsie*
6. *Airplane*
7. *Planes, Trains and Automobiles*
8. *Midnight Run*
9. *The Out-of-Towners*
10. *Big*

### Ten Great Films About Families

1. *Parenthood*
2. *Divine Secrets of the Ya-Ya Sisterhood*
3. *Cheaper by the Dozen*
4. *Rocket Gibraltar*
5. *Moonstruck*
6. *Hannah and Her Sisters*
7. *It's a Wonderful Life*
8. *The Sound of Music*
9. *Guess Who's Coming to Dinner*
10. *The Brothers McMullen*

### Ten Movies That Deal Positively with Aging

1. *Cocoon*
2. *The Straight Story*
3. *The Sunshine Boys*
4. *Space Cowboys*
5. *Grumpy Old Men*
6. *Used People*
7. *On Golden Pond*
8. The *Trip to Bountiful*
9. *Harold and Maude*
10. *Driving Miss Daisy*

▶ Surprise Mom with videotapes of her favorite old movies.

❧

---

### Ten Great Films About Fathers and Sons

1. *Field of Dreams*
2. *Kramer vs. Kramer*
3. *Indiana Jones and the Last Crusade*
4. *The Lion King*
5. *Life with Father*
6. *Life Is Beautiful*
7. *Searching for Bobby Fischer*
8. *Parenthood*
9. *Nothing in Common*
10. *A River Runs Through It*

### Ten Great Films About Mothers and Daughters

1. *Tumbleweeds*
2. *Postcards from the Edge*
3. *The Joy Luck Club*
4. *Secrets and Lies*
5. *Crossing Delancey* (grandmother/granddaughter)
6. *How to Make an American Quilt*
7. *Steel Magnolias*
8. *Little Women*
9. *Imitation of Life*
10. *Not Without My Daughter*

### Ten Great Films About Fathers and Daughters

1. *To Kill a Mockingbird*
2. *My Girl*
3. *A Little Princess*
4. *Fly Away Home*
5. *The Golden Bowl*
6. *Father of the Bride*
7. *Say Anything*
8. *A Bill of Divorcement*
9. *Eat Drink Man Woman*
10. *Paper Moon*

### Ten Great Films About Mothers and Sons

1. *Little Man Tate*
2. *Felicia's Journey*
3. *Riding in Cars with Boys*
4. *None but the Lonely Heart*
5. *Angela's Ashes*
6. *The Mating Season*
7. *The Yearling*
8. *The Sixth Sense*
9. *Mother*
10. *Dumbo*

Sing a song together. If you're really ambitious, try harmonizing.

Grow plants together. Discuss their progress.

If concentration is a problem, read children's books together and talk through the story instead of reading the text. Talk about the illustrations.

Anyone who has participated in Take Our Daughters (and Sons) to Work Day knows how rewarding the experience can be for everyone. How about designating a Take Our Parents to Work Day? Will it be difficult to explain your job to Dad, who's never touched a computer? Probably. Will Mom undermine your authority at work by telling everyone how cute you were as a baby? Maybe. Will it be a day long remembered for sharing interests and demonstrating a need to be in each other's lives? Definitely.

Get into the TV habit—discover soap operas.

❧

"Although I grew up hearing that my mind would rot if I watched too much TV, I do recall Mom being a 'General Hospital' fan when I was a kid. Of course, she certainly hadn't indulged herself in anything like that once she went back to teaching math. But here we are years later, and one day in the nursing home, we heard someone say something about Luke and Laura, and Mom immediately perked up. So I put the show on for her a few days later and was delighted to see her thoroughly enjoying her old passion. You can laugh about soap operas all you want to, but I can tell you I've seen the benefits: Mom is really curious to see what will happen to these people tomorrow, and she looks forward to 'her show.' Plus she has things to tell me about now that her own life has become relatively uneventful. Did you know that Luke and Laura are now contemplating their third wedding?"

*—Robin Rossner*

▶ Play ball. Even tossing a medium-sized inflatable ball back and forth with someone who is in a wheelchair can be fun, and it's excellent for strengthening reflexes.

## A Senior's Best Friend: The Joy of Pets

▶ Research shows that seniors who have pets are healthier (lower blood pressure, longer life span) and happier (lower stress). The right pet can provide a senior with companionship and stimulation, encourage exercise and a regular routine, and provide a sense of purpose and security.

▶ A number of nonprofit organizations are dedicated to bringing seniors and pets together, by sponsoring adoptions and providing support such as food, supplies, dog walking, and veterinary care for seniors with pets. Check with the local senior centers and humane societies in your area, or look for organizations online like petsforseniors.org.

▶ Don't immediately run out to get a dog. Consider what your senior's preferences, needs, abilities, and resources are before doing anything. Is he allergic to dander? Will he be able to walk the dog (even in snow) or is someone else available who can? And even if you're sure it will be a perfect match, don't surprise your loved one with a pet—it's not fair to Dad or to Rover. Discuss it first.

▶ Do two good turns at once. Rather than buying a trendy new breed, adopt for your senior an older pet in need of a home. Some humane societies even sponsor programs that match senior pets to senior people. Among the benefits of this choice is the fact that the animal is probably already trained and not so boisterous that it will overwhelm a senior.

▶ Know your mother's housing rights when it comes to her pets. Many seniors are forced to separate from their pets when circumstances force them to move. However, there are federal, state, and local laws that protect the rights of seniors and people with disabilities to keep pets in their homes. Don't let Mom give up her beloved pet until you've explored her legal options.

The number of pet-friendly senior care facilities is increasing as knowledge of the benefits of pet ownership increases. Look into these facilities when planning for your senior's care.

Service animals are exempt from "no pets" policies, and the categories of service animals are no longer just guide and hearing dogs but also include dogs or other animals that are specifically trained to help people cope with, and recover from, a variety of physical and mental illnesses such as stroke, epilepsy, and depression. The federal Fair Housing Act and your state and local civil rights laws have more information about animals that are necessary for a person's health, as well as definitions of who is protected to have pets or service animals in housing that has a no pets policy.

Encourage Dad to provide for his dog's future by making provisions in his will for the dog's care.

## Memories Old and New

Have the old family home movies transferred to video (your local video rental store can usually handle the job), and make sure your loved one knows how to operate the VCR. You will all enjoy countless memories together.

Make a scrapbook of letters, greeting cards, and other artifacts. Date everything and add explanatory captions. These books will be enjoyed for generations to come. If you're craft-minded, you know that scrapbooking has lately become a very popular craft. You can buy archival and handmade bindings, as well as various stickers and accessories that make the hobby fun even for the advanced craftsperson.

▶ Make a quilt or a fabric collage out of a parent's old clothing. What a wonderful way to recycle clothes that no longer fit or have become ruined for the most part.

▶ Take notes when the seniors in your life tell you stories, especially when they mention names.

▶ Ask your parent to help you make a time capsule of items that will give future generations a chance to touch the past.

▶ Plot your family tree. You can find computer software for sale or online to help you do it. Get family members to help, and share the finished product with all of them, even the ones you don't get along with.

▶ Put captions on photos.

෬෨

"The walls of our house were always covered with a photographic history of our lives. One of the saddest things about the onset of Alzheimer's was seeing Mom perplexed when she'd pass a photo because she was unable to recognize family members. So we put detailed captions on everything: 'Mom and Dad at our beach house in Ocracoke, July 1970'; 'John and Vivien are married at the First Baptist Church in Rumson, New Jersey, in 1983.' Not only did this help her (and the rest of us) identify the photos, but all together, they make an interesting history of our family."

—*Robert Castigano*

▸ Has Dad ever told you stories about serving in World War II? While some may not want to remember their war experience, most feel good talking about it. A natural time to bring it up might be Veterans Day or Memorial Day. Ask him to show you any medals, commendations, discharge papers, and so forth. Consider having them framed. More mature grandkids might be interested also, especially if they are studying history in school.

▸ Photo-processing shops and copy centers now offer many special graphics services. You can get life-sized cutouts of people, "talking" picture frames, T-shirts, mirrors, and calendars. Turn an ordinary photo into an event.

▸ Keep a diary of your visits with your parent.

෴

"One of the saddest things about seeing Dad lose his memory was the fact that he couldn't remember our visits, no matter how often we came. Sometimes, by the time I had driven home, there would be a message from him on the machine saying, 'How come you never come to see me anymore?' We solved the problem by installing a 'guest book' in his room at the nursing home. Each time we come, we write a sentence or two about what the day was like and how Dad was doing. Making the entries became an activity in itself, as we would sit together and decide how to describe the day. We're actually on our third notebook these days: the first two are crammed with notes and drawings that the kids did for Grampy; we even started pasting in greeting cards and other mementos, so the thing actually became our scrapbook. Most important, when Grampy forgets that his loved ones are always there for him, we ask him to open the book to the last entry. He sees the date and still doesn't recall the visit, but having evidence of it—in the form of a book of sweet memories—is comforting."

—*Theo Salavant*

Keep pictures around of your parents in better days. Let them know that in your heart, they will always be the vital, loving people who raised you.

Grandma might enjoy a newspaper from the day she was born (or came to this country, or got married) or a video that encapsulates a favorite year in history.

Photo-processing shops can restore old, damaged photos and make copies from your old prints.

If you tend to heavily annotate your calendars, keep old ones. They might help you recall some special days years from now.

Help your senior write thank-you notes, birthday cards, and so forth. Grandchildren will especially cherish these.

Keep a disposable camera ready at all times. You never know when you will want to capture a tender, precious moment.

Create an oral history. Focus on a subject or an area your parents know a lot about.

Replace bad memories with good ones.

☾☽

"We dreaded the holidays—Dad passed away the day after Christmas last year, and we knew the memories would depress Mom. So we made a really special dinner this year. Everyone showed up, which is a real rarity, and during dessert we said a special prayer and then each member of the family talked about their funniest memory of Dad, and the day became a celebration of his life. We've promised Mom we'll do this every year, and I know she'll look forward to it."

—*Janice Gerber*

▸ Date all photos. (Don't rely on your own memory to date them later. Remember, you won't be young forever!) Don't put paste on the backs of photos that have information on them.

▸ Photograph seniors at *their* eye level.

▸ Throw a reunion for your senior. It doesn't have to be a huge party celebrating fifty years of anything—it can be a small dessert party for people who used to live in the neighborhood or those who might have belonged to the same bridge club.

▸ Talk to Dad about the good things he will be remembered for when he is gone, assuming he talks openly about death.

▸ Your mother may enjoy taking a course in journal writing, which will help her organize her history, structure her stories, and get started.

▸ Time lines are great for illustrating history, whether it's the history of your family or a journal of everything that's happened in the past month.

ை

"Maybe because it was my favorite project in the fourth grade—or maybe I'm 'historically challenged'—but I've always used time lines the way some people use lists. Mom and Dad love the 'assignments' I give them: I recently asked them for a time line of the years before we kids were born. I know they have fun doing these, and it gives them plenty of reasons to reminisce. I keep these in a folder and share them with others in the family from time to time. I know I'll cherish these always."

—*Barry Longeri*

Photographs can be printed onto fabric. If you're talented enough to be able to make clothing, this might give you some ideas for unusual designs. You can also dry-transfer photos onto most cotton fabrics using the kits sold at craft stores.

Ask your parents to help you make lists about your family: the best parties you had at the house in Connecticut, your pets, places you spent summers, the best vacations you ever took, and so on. Keep these together in a special place.

You know those dusty boxes with piles and envelopes and folders of old photos no one seems to care about? *Care about them!* Make it a family project—consider yourselves detectives. Organize the photos and get family members to help identify and date them all. Then put them in albums chronologically or by subject. Keep all the photos you can't identify in a separate file. Bring them to family reunions or E-mail them to family members who can provide dates, names, and places.

Don't stop taking photographs of your parents just because they don't look as spiffy as they used to or because one of them has become frail. You can always retouch the photos if you feel you need to.

༄༅

"It was so frustrating to go back to all the photos of Mom and Dad taken over decades just to find one great portrait of the two of them and see that in all the photos where Dad looked good, Mom's eyes were closed. If Mom's eyes happened to be open, guess what? Dad's head was turned. John was able to scan two photos taken at the same time into the computer and switch heads so that I now have a perfect portrait that the whole family seems to truly appreciate."

—*Toni Cella*

If friends and family are scattered over long distances, make an audiotape or a videotape of your parents and send it around, chain-letter style. Or send an audiotape to everyone and ask each person to add a short greeting. Your parents will love hearing the whole family "together."

Who knew that immortality only costs $48? For that price, you can have a star named after your loved one. Visit internationalstar registry.com or write to the International Star Registry at 34523 Wilson Road, Ingleside, IL 60041.

Surround your seniors with the trappings of their own memories, even if they're ones you don't share in. Make sure they have easy access to the books, letters, and photos that may mean so much to them.

Make a collage or shadowbox of photos and artifacts showing your parent in all the activities he used to be involved in. It's a great way for him to share his life with visitors.

Learn your parents' language, especially if they speak a dying language or one you won't be able to learn more about after they're gone.

❧

"Rachel and I were embarrassed, as children, by the fact that our parents spoke a whole different language and that when they did speak English, they talked with 'funny' accents. Funny that today we take so much pride in the Yiddish that seems to be in our blood; we converse in our 'mother's tongue' all the time now, and we're shocked at how much of the language we retained despite ourselves."

—Ann Hertzman

Clean your attic while your parents can still remember the stories about all that old junk. Those old skates with the price tag still on might have a story behind them, and the weird hat collection might have belonged to an eccentric relative you never even knew you had.

Offer to keep a journal for your parents. They can dictate their entries, and you can agree not to interrupt or ask questions until they're done with the entry. If your parents have a story to tell that is of historical significance, consider donating it to a museum or project that collects such memoirs. The Holocaust Museum in Washington, D.C., for example, collects information about Holocaust survivors.

Make scrapbooks with themes: Christmas, summer vacations, school pictures. Photos have stories to tell; look at them in different combinations and sequences. Sometimes the stories change.

Your days of caregiving may be among the best memories you have after your loved ones have passed. Take notice of all the good moments and of the love that passes between you at this special time.

Once in a while, ask your loved one to tell you the history of objects you may have taken for granted your whole life.

&

"I had no idea that the bowl I've been keeping my loose change in all these years was brought here from Germany by my grandmother! We treat it with a lot more respect since Mom casually mentioned this last time she was here."

—*Lorraine Ferber*

## The Rest of the Family

If you are the primary caregiver, make an effort to include other family members in taking on some responsibility, even if you don't feel you need the help. For one thing, it's better to get others involved *before* your senior's needs change and/or you max out—both likely occurrences—and before everyone gets used to and comes to expect having you do all the work.

Organize a family meeting to work out a plan for caregiving, even if your father is thriving independently. It's better to share concerns and opinions—especially to hear those from Dad—early on. Have the meeting at his home, and put him in the driver's seat as much as possible. The main goal is to make sure everyone in the family knows and understands Dad's wishes.

Take advantage of the strengths of different family members and the unique relationship each has with your mother. The logic she uses in deciding whom she asks for help may not make perfect sense to you—your brother is a doctor, but Mom counts on you to communicate with health care staff, and you're a CPA, but she thinks of your brother (the former junior-high math whiz) when balancing her checkbook—but her comfort and trust are more important.

Include a long-distance sibling in the caregiving process by keeping her informed—without making her feel guilty for not being there.

If you are a long-distance caregiver, respect the frustrations of sib-lings who live closer. Let them know that although you can't be there as much as you'd like, you share the load emotionally.

Help your parents maintain relationships with their grandchildren. If they have problems using the phone, call relatives together when you go to visit. Schedule activities that the little ones will enjoy on days when they come to visit (trips to the zoo, a storytelling hour). Similarly, make appropriate plans on days when older kids are around. Make sure that even the littlest ones get to spend time with your loved one; you have no way of knowing what they will remember as they grow older—one hug can be remembered for a lifetime.

Make an audiotape of your parent reading a bedtime story and play it for your child.

Encourage kids to share their hobbies and interests with their grandparents.

Separate your personal issues with family members from the tasks at hand. If you can't stand your uppity Aunt Susan but seeing her makes Dad happy, take a deep breath and put your feelings aside.

Relate to siblings outside of parental needs. Whether it's about your children, your love lives, baseball, or the stock market, try to connect with one another on more than just one level.

༄

"Kathi and I were always close, but we were being so diligent about staying on top of Mom and Dad's move to a retirement community that we pretty much started ignoring each other. One day I realized it had been months since we'd talked about anything but them; I had no idea what was going on in her life. We make it a point now to get together once every few weeks to talk only about ourselves, an indulgence that makes us both stronger and much more able to deal with the workload."

—*Geri Kamens*

Don't be the intermediary in your family. When people need to communicate with each other, encourage them to do it directly.

The less you see your mother, the more pronounced her deterioration is likely to appear. Expect family members who have less frequent contact to be surprised or upset when this occurs, and try to prepare them for changes when possible.

Tell long-distance siblings exactly what you expect from them. Mention concrete things you would like them to do to help; this will avoid misunderstanding and resentment.

If you need to present Dad with a new plan for his care, agree on it with siblings before you spring it on him. This way you can settle arguments beforehand, and you'll appear as a united front.

Demonstrate your care of your parent to your own children. Let them see just how tenderly this job can be done. You'll teach them more about responsibility and caring through your behavior than your words. Remember that they may be using what they learn on you someday.

Learn to forgive and forget. Old feuds and resentments can only adversely affect your caregiving. If you and your siblings have never gotten along, the onset of your parents' senior years is an excellent time to air (or put aside) your feelings and then pledge to move on.

If long-distance siblings don't get the message about the fact that your loved one needs help, make a videotape of your parent that will convey the point.

Give each member of the family who may be overseeing your mother a copy of her living will. You can reduce it on a copy machine and keep a wallet-sized copy with you always. You can enlarge it again when you need to.

If family members are going to be impacted by any decision you make, they should be in on making the decision. This includes the kids. Even if they don't have a "full vote," they're more likely to cooperate if they were involved from the start.

Encourage older kids to talk about specific ways in which they want to help out.

Don't try to take over a healthy parent's role in caring for a dependent parent. You can support them as much as they (and you) are comfortable with, but remember that they are still making the decisions and running the show.

Encourage a caregiving parent to delegate responsibility to others, including hired help, when possible.

Support outside activity for your caregiving parent. Encourage Dad to keep going to his weekly poker game while you or another trusted caregiver stays with Mom.

Have quality time alone together. Take Mom for a pedicure while Dad is at the senior day care program.

Look into support groups for older caregivers. If they are having a really tough time, they may need individual therapy.

Offer to help in specific ways.

❧

"I was always asking Mom what I could do to help with Dad, but she always said, 'Nothing, dear, we're fine,' even though I knew she was struggling. Now I've learned to offer to do specific things, like take him to his doctor visits. She accepts my help a lot more that way."

—*Pat Conti*

Pay attention to your caregiving parent's health. With everyone focusing on the less functioning spouse, the caregiving spouse's health problems can go unnoticed.

Caregivers are at higher risk for depression and substance abuse. Look out for signs of both.

# 9

# Getting Help from Other Caregivers

∾

## "Help" Is Not a Four-Letter Word

It's been stated before but bears repeating: consider hiring a geriatric caseworker who can help you determine what kind of regular professional help you can use in caring for your senior.

Supportive care options include facilities and programs to which your senior will go, such as senior centers and adult day care programs, and services that will come to your senior, such as meal delivery, reassurance visits, and home care. Services are provided professionally and on a volunteer basis.

If you primarily care for your senior at home but could use a break periodically, the Senior Corps (1-800-424-8867 or seniorcorps.org) will provide a trained volunteer to come and stay with her once a week. Local religious groups may offer similar volunteer help.

▶ Contact the Eldercare Locator (1-800-677-1116) or the National Association for Home Care (1-202-547-7424) for information about professional care for your senior. Other information resources include local senior centers and religious organizations.

▶ If Mom mainly needs company and activity, she may be fine spending her days at a senior center, many of which will pick her up, provide lunch, and drop her off at home at the end of the day.

▶ Adult day care programs are a compromise between living at home and full-time assisted living for seniors who need supervised care. In a typical program, a van will pick up your father at about 9 A.M.; drive him to a facility where he will socialize, have lunch, engage in activities, and possibly receive routine medical care; and then drop him off at home around 5 P.M.

▶ Ideally, an adult day care program has one supervisor for each six clients, four if the clients are very impaired. The program should also have a social worker and registered nurse on staff.

▶ If you are going away, are temporarily unavailable, or just need a break, you can arrange for professional respite care. This temporary care service can be provided at home or in a nursing facility. Check with your local Area Agency on Aging or any home health care service.

▶ Give your senior time to adjust to anything new.

෬

---

"My father hated the idea of going to a day program. I was really surprised at how much he got to like it after a while."

—*Deb Ingalls*

Grandma will be more likely to enjoy a program that offers the right activities—something that interests her *and* suits her abilities.

Does your local high school offer courses in home economics? The school might give credit to a student for helping you care for your loved one.

All home care is not equal. Options range from having a caregiver live in the home full-time, to rotating several workers who live outside the home, to having part-time help for when you are not available or need a rest. The type of care you arrange will also depend on your senior's needs, whether it is housekeeping, personal care, or medical supervision. Contact your local Area Agency on Aging for information on the different levels of care available to you.

When hiring caregivers, check references carefully. Personal recommendations are best. When speaking with past employers, ask about the biggest mistake the person ever made, especially if the caregiver is getting a glowing overall report. No one's perfect.

Call elder care agencies in the morning, when they seem to have a lot more time to give you their attention.

Don't let any caregiver just "take over"; your senior should remain in charge as much as possible while getting necessary help.

Be clear from the beginning as to your expectations of a caregiver. Be specific about duties: answering the phone, watering the plants, handling mail, dealing with pets, shopping, cooking, and so on. Also, find out about the caregiver's expectations for the job. What tasks are they trained to do? Are there tasks that they cannot (or will not) do?

Dad will no doubt have complaints about his caregivers, and some of these complaints may be quite serious. You need to take all complaints seriously. Even if the exact version your father gives you may turn out to be only part of the story, your investigating will assure him that he is being respected, and caregivers will know that you are paying close attention.

If you've accused a caregiver of bad behavior and it turns out you were wrong, let him know. This is really important. Good caregivers take pride in their work, and being wrongly accused of something can be devastating to anyone.

Consider using one of the many concealed video "nanny cams" that are on the market.

Make sure caregivers understand your instructions. Don't just write them on notes; discuss them as well to make sure the instructions are clear and to determine agreement.

If you are supposed to relieve a caregiver and you're running late, always notify her. Have a backup plan in case this happens. Remember that the caregiver has a life and possibly a family, too.

Make out (private) "report cards" for each of the caregivers you hire so you can refer to these later if you need them. If there's something a caregiver does especially well, note that. Keep notes on the objections you had to prospective caregivers you didn't hire.

Have regular meetings with all caregiving staff. If there is more than one caregiver, you'll be better off if they know one another and can communicate, especially when there are scheduling problems. Now and then try to extend the hours of one or another so that they overlap. They might have a lot to teach each other.

▶ Make sure your father is familiar with anyone who will take care of him. Dad should always have a say in who cares for him. Remember that caregiving can be a very intimate process. It will all go best if you agree up front on the personnel involved, to the extent that that's possible. At a minimum, introduce caregivers to Dad before they actually begin work.

▶ During the holidays, remember any paid caregivers (nursing home aides, day care workers, shuttle drivers, etc.) who help make your senior's life better. Make sure that your gifts are thoughtful and generous.

▶ Let caregivers see photos of your parent in earlier days. Caregivers and others will more easily connect with her if they are reminded of the vitality she once had.

◌

---

"A year after cousin Pauline was diagnosed with Alzheimer's, Maureen came to live with her and Joe, Pauline's husband. Maureen was a dedicated, caring professional, but Joe is not the easiest person to live with—he tends to withdraw and then appears hostile even if he's not. We were afraid we'd lose Maureen, and she was a real gem. One day, I went over there for dinner and I got Joe to take out photos of Pauline back when we all went on vacations together and Pauline would win every swimming race we ever had. Maureen was touched that Joe was sharing these with her and surprised when he started going on and on about the old days—talking a mile a minute, saying more to her than he had in all the weeks she'd been working there. Things were a little different after that. For one thing, I think Maureen looked at Pauline with a new kind of respect. She also was a lot more understanding of just how much of a vivacious, energetic person Joe was missing."

*—Beth Castigano*

▶ Call at various times a day to check on your parent and on the caregiver. Don't allow your calls (or visits) to become predictable. Showing up at unexpected times is a good idea, especially in the beginning. Of course, you don't have to say you're there to check up. Invent an excuse to drop by.

▶ If you're doing something nice for your parent (baking something special, picking up a small gift), consider doing the same for the caregiver.

▶ If Grandpa is embarrassed about his nursing companion in front of the friends he encounters when he goes out for his walk, tell him to introduce the companion as "my friend." The real nature of the relationship is no one's business.

▶ Create a checklist of issues (e.g., temperature, breathing problems, medication) and ask each caregiver to fill out a column before they go off duty.

▶ Caregivers provide your family with so many of the resources you need to keep your life and that of your parent vital. How much do you know about their families?

▶ Make sure a home caregiver is comfortable in your home, that she knows she's welcome in the kitchen, on the patio, and so forth. Would a small refrigerator or microwave in the room she occupies (or elsewhere around the house) make her job easier?

▶ Be realistic in your expectations for caregivers. Don't expect more of other people than you could ever do for yourself. In fact, accept that no paid caregivers, no matter how dedicated, are going to care as much as you do, and you will never be 100 percent satisfied with their care.

# HOME AWAY FROM HOME:
## ASSISTED-LIVING FACILITIES

▶ Hunting for an appropriate facility for your senior can be among the most traumatic experiences you will face in your life. The emotional end of it can be overwhelming; the financial and business end of it can make your head spin. Hire a geriatric care manager to help you through the maze of paperwork and choices. You can locate geriatric care managers in your area through your local Area Agency on Aging. To find geriatric care managers online or to learn whether your parent is eligible for free geriatric care management, contact Living Strategies (1-877-244-6443 or livingstrategies.com) or the National Association of Professional Geriatric Care Managers (1-520-881-8008 or caremanager.org).

▶ Senior care facilities usually have waiting lists. Learn about which of these facilities are available to you before you actually need them. Know that they come in all shapes and sizes.

▶ Common fears seniors experience in entering assisted living include loneliness, neglect or abuse, and loss of dignity. Listen to your senior's concerns and discuss how you will address them. Most of these fears can be allayed by researching facilities beforehand, developing a plan for monitoring when your senior is in residence, and sharing your plans and information with your senior.

ᐤᎧᎧ

"I was shocked at how receptive Dad was to the nursing home. Mom would have hated it—it's small and you get almost no privacy. But he loves the intimacy and says it always makes him feel safe to hear the sound of other voices."

—*Miriam Gans*

If you promised your parents you would never put them in a nursing home but find now that circumstances prevent you from keeping that promise, remind your parent often how things have changed and why this is necessary. Talk about the fact that years back, when you made that promise, the well-run, clean, safe, and cheerful nursing homes that abound today were rare. Remind them that you will still be there for them, just as you are now.

You'll need an attorney to go over contracts, check the legitimacy of fees and pricing schedules, and alert you to your rights as well as those of your parents. You'll save plenty on the lawyer's hourly rate if you choose one with plenty of experience in elder care.

Your local Area Agency on Aging will send you a list of facilities available in your state. Visit any that are possibilities and even a few that aren't.

The very best way to judge a facility is to ask yourself one important question: how would *you* feel about living there?

You can get a copy of the most recent inspection report on any nursing home facility in the country by contacting your local Medicare office or visiting medicare.gov.

Visit facilities at various times of day.

⟩⟨

"The daytime staff at my father's first nursing home was fantastic—really caring and personable. Then I visited one time at night—what a difference! The little staff that were around were unmotivated and unhelpful. We switched, and I visited the second one at night beforehand."

—*Christine Sommers*

There are assisted-living facilities that provide multitiered levels of care for senior residents according to their needs and as their needs change:

- Residents live self-sufficiently in an apartment or a town house within the assisted-living community (Tier 1).
- Residents live in an apartment or a private room where services such as meals, housekeeping, and medication supervision are provided (Tier 2).
- Residents receive nursing home care with twenty-four-hour supervision (Tier 3).

This arrangement avoids the stress and disruption involved in displacing seniors and/or their surviving spouses as their needs change.

Every nursing home is assigned a long-term care ombudsman employed by the state's Area Agency on Aging. It's the ombudsman's job to monitor the home for abuse or neglect and to mediate relations between staff, residents, and families. Contact the nursing home's ombudsman with your questions and concerns.

Especially when your mother first enters the facility, it's important to let her know you're there for her while at the same time stepping back and giving her a chance to bond with her new surroundings. Often, feelings of guilt cause us to be overprotective.

Make friends with other residents, and tell them all about your parent. Especially if Dad is modest about the fact that he was once the top Latin dancer in the country, he may attract new friends he wouldn't make on his own.

It takes about six weeks to get used to a roommate. Don't be surprised if you find Grandpa adjusting to a personality you never dreamed would mesh with his. Sometimes opposites get along best, since they have fewer territorial and power issues.

If possible, have a friend go with you to check out a place that you're seriously considering. A friend's caring but less personally attached perspective will come in handy.

Get to know someone in each department at the facility. Make friends with the guy in the kitchen, the lady who manages the laundry, the gardener, the hairdresser, the housekeeping people. They're all members of your new family.

It usually takes residents six months to get used to living in a senior facility. Give it time. But if you're sure that everything points to the fact that this is the wrong place for Mom, get her out and find a more appropriate place.

Edit your senior's medical diary to create a condensed version that might be of interest to the nursing home personnel.

Holidays don't have to be celebrated all in one day. If you're from a large family, you might not want to overwhelm Grandpa with too many visitors at one time. Organize the family into well-spaced visits, and take a whole week or month, for instance, to celebrate Thanksgiving.

If someone is treating your parent in a way that you think is wrong or which you don't understand, ask questions before you accuse.

෧෨

---

"I went crazy when I heard Patsy, who takes care of Mom, yelling at her at the top of her lungs as I walked in the room. But when I pulled the curtain, Mom was sitting there smiling up at Patsy as she struggled to get her hearing aid on!"

—*Murial Behar*

▶ One gift at a time is better than a barrage of presents. Be mindful of the limited space your loved one has available.

▶ Think about how you will structure your visit before you go. If two activities are planned, make sure you have time for each. Have a backup plan or two—and go armed with plenty of flexibility. Try not to show your disappointment if your parent prefers to rest quietly instead of going on the elaborate picnic you planned.

▶ Keep your loved one aware of the passage of time. Mark off the days on a calendar as they pass, and decorate the room as various holidays approach.

▶ Make Grandma's room (or her half of the room) as homey as possible. If all of her favorite things just won't fit, bring in a few and then replace them with others as the seasons change. Seeing missed objects will be like seeing old friends.

▶ Send mail often, even if you visit in person. Seniors love to get mail, especially if they get to read it in front of their friends and share any good news.

▶ If your parent is placed in an activity group that you think is inappropriate, give it some time before you intervene.

∽

"Mom in a volleyball group? This is a woman who hated sports with a passion. As it turns out, their version of 'volleyball' involves throwing a ball around from one person to another, and she doesn't seem to mind it at all. In fact, she enjoys the company and even boasts about her new involvement in 'sports.'"

—*Syl Faerber*

▸ Each time you visit, (surreptitiously) check Mom's skin for irritations that may lead to bedsores. Massages are not only a good way to prevent bedsores, but they also provide some great shared moments of intimacy.

▸ Be your father's advocate. Let him know that you are there to fight for him at times when he can't fight for himself. Make sure he knows that you will always defend him and that you are always going to be there for him.

▸ Get to know every member of the staff, and address them by their names. Let them know who you are. Before you address anyone on the staff, introduce yourself, even if you think they should know your name by now.

▸ Keep notes on your visits. A history of specific complaints might come in handy down the road.

▸ Don't dismiss complaints just because they sound absurd.

❧

"Dad kept complaining about the snakes that were under his bed—he could see them come running out every morning. I searched under the bed and even convinced him that there was poison under there, but the 'snakes' persisted. One morning I was helping him get breakfast, and Sylvia, who mops the floor every morning, came in and started mopping up around the bed. Dad went ballistic. 'There they are again!' he shouted. It was the mop, as it turned out. With Dad so groggy in the morning, I could now see how easily he was confused. I've asked Sylvia to hold off on releasing the 'snakes' until after Dad is up and dressed. It worked!"

—*Elvie Nadell*

▶ If your parent has a favorite way of doing something, don't be shy about telling the staff, no matter how "silly" the routine might seem. A favorite cup, the company of a teddy bear, or a special way of saying goodnight can make life seem normal again for a senior whose life has been uprooted.

▶ If Dad objects and becomes dejected when your visit is over, know that he will most likely recover soon after you're gone. It may help your peace of mind to call later and ask a staff member how he is doing. While you're guiltily picturing Dad staring out a window, pining away for you, he's probably absorbed in a game or TV program.

▶ The housekeeping service usually takes care of everything. But if there are certain pieces of clothing that require special care and would be better off handled at your local dry cleaner, let the housekeeping department know and write the instruction ("hold for home laundry") right on the label.

▶ If lots of people are visiting, they shouldn't all leave at the same time. Being left behind by a crowd can be devastating for your senior, no matter how much fun the visit was.

▶ Many senior facilities make it possible for residents to attend neighboring colleges and take adult education courses off the premises. Find out if that's a possibility.

⌒

"We've had lots and lots of wonderful family parties here—we have birthdays and holiday dinners, and we even had a couple get married here once. But when Miriam Snyder got her college diploma, her graduation party was the best yet. She was seventy-three!"

*—Simon Hirsch*

▶ Lots of short phone calls throughout the day are better than one long one. Organize your family into a phone brigade.

▶ Urge your mother to volunteer her services. Even seniors with mobility and other problems can help in the library, in crafts rooms, and at game time.

▶ We predict that ten years from now, wheelchairs will come equipped with special compartments for laptop computers, since every senior will know the value of being wired. For now, start out slowly, be patient during lessons, and limit your instruction to basics until Dad gets the knack of it.

▶ If tipping isn't allowed, don't tip. The temptation to accept your offer might get someone in trouble. Find other ways of letting staff members know how much you appreciate them. Write letters of commendation to the management of the facility.

▶ No matter how plush the nursing home or how modern the facility, the staff is going to be overworked. Help out when you can.

▶ If Mom's favorite paintings just won't fit on the limited wall space she now has, consider donating them to the home or facility so that she can enjoy them more than she ever has before—by sharing them with others.

၆⃝⁀၅

---

"She is so proud to see others admire the painting she's loved all these years, and we were all touched by the sentiment she asked us to add to the inscription under the painting: 'A shared blessing is a double blessing.'"

—*Sue Weinberg*

Senior facilities change hands often. If you liked one you saw last year, don't assume it's still in the same condition. New owners often mean new policies.

Go to every meeting to which you're invited at least once. Having a parent in a nursing home can easily become a part-time job for you. Organize the brigade—ask others to attend meetings for you and report back. If you can't attend, can someone tape the discussion for you?

Your senior may greatly benefit from having a small refrigerator for snacks and a TV and VCR. Rotate his movie collection often.

Let the staff know the conditions under which you want to be notified. Some facilities won't call you if your parent falls, for instance, unless you tell them to do so.

Arrange to take your parent outdoors as much as possible when you visit. No matter how well staffed the facility is, it's usually impossible to get everyone outside on those gorgeous spring days. Unfortunately, in the scheme of nursing care, this is generally not considered a priority.

Be honest with your parent about how long she'll be there.

ᏄᏫ

"That is the worst thing I see families do to the residents. They lie and say, 'Oh, Mommy, you will only be here for a few days.' Then the family goes home and the resident thinks we are crazy because we act like she will be living here. When she finds out the truth, she is mad and doesn't know who she can trust anymore."

—*Kayleen Sutherland*

In addition to the obvious, here are some questions you might ask yourself when reviewing an assisted-living facility:

- Do staff members refer to residents by name?
- Will you be able to have private time with your parent when you come to visit?
- What's the food really like? Eat a whole meal there!
- How many of the caregivers you see on the unit are privately hired and how many are members of the staff?
- Are visiting hours limited? Why?
- How often will your senior have a chance to go outdoors?
- What sorts of care does this facility provide that may not be necessary now but which may become needed in the future?
- Would *you* like to live there?

# 10

# Taking Care of You

⟨∿⟩

## Staying Balanced, Staying Strong

▸Don't neglect your own needs. Remember those airplane safety movies that instruct you to put your own oxygen mask on first, before assisting a child or someone else who needs help? The logic is that you won't be much help to anyone else if you're disoriented or passed out yourself, and it applies to a lot of areas in life.

▸If you're a control freak, this is a good time to work on changing your ways. Take advantage of all offers to help you in caring for your senior. Remember that the value here is not only to you but also to the giver, who becomes empowered and will therefore be more involved in the long run.

▸If support groups aren't your style, consider seeking therapy or counseling to preserve your own emotional and mental well-being. If you work outside your home, check to see if your employer provides support and counseling for these issues—some of the large companies do.

▶ Always keep your own limitations in mind. You can help your loved ones; you cannot save their lives. Remember what your role really is.

▶ Delegate responsibilities when possible. You can't do it all. Involve other family members, volunteers, and professional help.

▶ Join a support group for caregivers. Your local Area Agency on Aging, senior centers, and Eldercare Locator (1-800-677-1116) will all have information on groups in your area. Some may specifically address issues that you're dealing with, such as Alzheimer's.

▶ Check out one of the many online communities for caregivers of the elderly. Many have forums, message boards, and chat rooms that serve as virtual support groups.

▶ If you're an adult child, check to see if Children of Aging Parents (CAPS), a peer group providing information and support, has a chapter in your area. Call 1-800-227-7294 or visit caps4caregivers.org.

▶ Avoid comparing yourself to other caregivers. Since you're looking from the outside, it's all too easy to focus on their strengths while being painfully aware of all of your own imperfections.

▶ Understand that it's normal to sometimes feel angry or resentful toward your loved one and to have unkind thoughts about her. Try not to feel guilty about such thoughts. After all, thoughts are just thoughts—it's what you do that counts.

༄

"When I catch myself having angry thoughts about my mother, I feel guilty, like I'm a bad son. Then I think of a reverse situation: what if I always thought really nice things about my mother but didn't *do* anything to help her. Would I be a good son?"

—*Noah Levin*

▸ Practice stress-reduction techniques such as yoga, meditation, and deep breathing. Even fifteen minutes every morning can make a difference. *Total Relaxation: Healing Practices for Body, Mind & Spirit*, by John Harvey, provides clear and simple instruction, including a CD to guide you through.

▸ If you're feeling guilty or self-critical, try imagining a caring friend whom you admire in your same position. Would you think she'd deserve such criticism? What would you say to her to help her get a better perspective?

▸ Explain to your friends what you are going through; let them know you need their patience. The ones who don't understand are not really your friends—don't waste your time feeling guilty about them.

▸ Alcohol may seem like a good temporary comfort for the burden you have as a caregiver, and it's fairly common for caregivers to develop problems with alcohol—be careful not to overdo it. Try taking a walk or a bath, listening to music, or talking to someone instead.

▸ Make a commitment to doing at least one special thing just for you every week and *stick to it*.

⟲

"My sister and I are both very involved in taking care of our parents (Dad has Alzheimer's, and Mom is recovering from a stroke). Once a week, no matter what, she goes for a manicure, and I spend an hour at a shooting range. It's such a little thing, but it's a way for each of us to recharge our batteries. And since it's all too easy to shortchange yourself, we check in with each other to make sure we're really doing it."

—*Candy Andretti*

If friends or other family members offer to help, give them a choice of *specific* things they can do for you.

Your role as a caregiver is important, but don't let it take over your identity. Remember that you are still a wife (or husband), a friend, an animal lover, a film buff . . . and act accordingly.

Learn to let things go. Does your own house really need to be that clean? Can you get someone else to do Thanksgiving dinner this year? Do you really have to have the curtains washed that often?

If you absolutely can't leave your parent and you need a break, can you take a vacation together? Consider bringing along another person for sitting and relieving you so you can have some time for yourself.

Practice your faith. Use the extensive support—spiritual, practical, and emotional—provided by your religious community.

Instead of feeling guilty about things you can't do, ask yourself what you can do *now*.

When your role as a caregiver comes to an end, consider volunteering and using your new skills to help others.

∾

## Twelve Steps for Caregivers

1. Although I cannot control the disease process, I need to remember I can control many aspects of how it affects me and my relative.
2. I need to take care of myself so that I can continue doing the things that are most important.
3. I need to simplify my lifestyle so that my time and energy are available for things that are really important at this time.
4. I need to cultivate the gift of allowing others to help me, because caring for my relative is too big a job to be done by one person.
5. I need to take one day at a time rather than worry about what may or may not happen in the future.
6. I need to structure my day because a consistent schedule makes life easier for me and my relative.
7. I need to have a sense of humor because laughter helps to put things in a more positive perspective.
8. I need to remember that my relative is not being "difficult" on purpose; rather, his/her behavior and emotions are distorted by the illness.
9. I need to focus on and enjoy what my relative can still do rather than constantly lament over what is gone.
10. I need to increasingly depend upon other relationships for love and support.
11. I need to frequently remind myself that I am doing the best that I can at this very moment.
12. I need to draw upon the Higher Power which I believe is available to me.

*By Carol J. Farran, D.N.Sc., R.N., and Eleanora Keane-Hagerty, M.A.*

# Final Words

〜

One of the most rewarding things about being a caregiver—on any level—is the lessons to which we are constantly treated. We hope that's something you can celebrate.

Just as important are the teachers who offer us these lessons. Know that while you may be a student at this stage of your life, as time passes, you are likely to become the voice of experience. We urge you to share your stories and thoughts about elder care with people around you. Your friends and acquaintances may not always want to hear every detail of your ordeal, but ingenious solutions and useful ideas empower us all and help elevate the quality of elder care that we expect for our loved ones and, ultimately, for ourselves.

If you would like to contribute tips or ideas for future volumes of this book, please send snail mail to us at:

The Caregiver's Essential Handbook
Box 74
Haworth, NJ 07641

# Resources

∽

We have listed here the methods by which the contacts mentioned throughout the book are most easily reached.

**AARP (formerly the American Association of Retired Persons)**
601 E Street NW
Washington, DC 20049
1-800-424-3410
aarp.org

**Abledata**
abledata.com

**All Devices Network**
190 West Continental Road
#220-233
Green Valley, AZ 85614
1-866-674-3549
alldevices.net

**American Geriatrics Society**
Empire State Building
350 Fifth Avenue
Suite 801
New York, NY 10118
1-212-308-1414
americangeriatrics.org
(refers callers to local services)

**American Medical Identifications**
4001 North Shepherd
Suite 100
Houston, TX 77018
1-800-363-5985
americanmedical-id.com

**American Red Cross**
National Headquarters
430 17th Street NW
Washington, DC 20006
1-866-GET-INFO (1-866-438-4636)
redcross.org

**American Sleep Apnea Association**
1424 K Street NW
Suite 302
Washington, DC 20005
1-202-293-3650
sleepapnea.org

**American Sleep Disorders Association**
One Westbrook Corporate Center
Suite 920
Westchester, IL 60154
1-708-492-0930
asda.org

**Better Business Bureau**
4200 Wilson Boulevard
Suite 800
Arlington, VA 22203-1838
1-703-276-0100
bbb.org

**B Independent**
905 Warren Way
Richardson, TX 75080
1-913-390-0247
bindependent.com

**Caring Concepts**
1-800-336-2660
caringconcepts.com

**Caring for an Aging Parent**
thirdage.com
(online instruction)

**Centers for Disease Control and Prevention**
1600 Clifton Road
Atlanta, GA 30333
1-404-639-3311
cdc.gov

**Children of Aging Parents (CAPS)**
609 Woodbourne Road
Suite 302A
Levittown, PA 19057
1-800-227-7294
caps4caregivers.org
(refers callers to local services)

**DMA Mail Preference Service**
PO Box 643
Carmel, NY 10512
the-dma.org

**DMA Telephone Preference Service**
PO Box 1559
Carmel, NY 10512
the-dma.org

**Elderhostel**
75 Federal Street
Boston, MA 02110-1941
1-877-426-8056
1-617-426-8056
elderhostel.org

International Association for Medical
   Assistance to Travellers
417 Center Street
Lewiston, NY 14092
1-716-754-4883
iamat.org

IRS Tax Assistance
1-888-227-7669

Lighthouse International
111 East 59th Street
New York, NY 10022-1202
1-800-829-0500
lighthouse.org

Medicare Hotline
1-800-633-4227
medicare.gov

Medic Care, Inc.
1-561-748-0840
mediccareinc.com

National Alzheimer's Association
919 North Michigan Avenue
Suite 1100
Chicago, IL 60611-1676
1-800-272-3900
1-312-335-8700
alz.org

National Association of Area
   Agencies on Aging
Eldercare Locator
1-800-677-1116
n4a.org
(connects callers with their local Area
Agency on Aging)

National Association for Home Care
   (NAHC)
228 Seventh Street SE
Washington, DC 20003
1-202-547-7424
nahc.org

National Association for Professional
   Geriatric Care Managers
1604 North Country Club Road
Tucson, AZ 85716-3102
1-520-881-8008
1-877-244-6443
caremanager.org

National Association for the Visually
   Handicapped
22 West 21st Street
New York, NY 10010
1-212-255-2804
1-212-889-3141
or
3201 Balboa Street
San Francisco, CA 94121
1-415-221-3201

National Foundation for Depressive
   Illness
PO Box 2257
New York, NY 10116
1-800-239-1264
1-800-248-4344
health.gov

National Fraud Information Center
PO Box 65868
Washington, DC 20035
1-800-876-7060
fraud.org

**National Institute of Mental Health**
6001 Executive Boulevard
Room 8184, MSC 9663
Bethesda, MD 20892-9663
1-301-443-4513
nimh.nih.gov

**National Mental Health Association**
1021 Prince Street
Alexandria, VA 22314-2971
1-800-969-6642
nmha.org

**National Senior Games
   Association**
PO Box 82059
Baton Rouge, LA 70884
1-225-766-6800
nsga.com

**Senior Corps**
1-800-424-8867
seniorcorps.org

**Service Corps of Retired
   Executives**
1-800-634-0245

**Silvert's**
3280 Steeles Avenue West
Suite 18
Concord (Toronto), Ontario L4K 2Y2
Canada
1-800-387-7088
1-905-738-4545
silverts.com

**Social Security Administration**
Office of Public Inquiries
6401 Security Boulevard
Room 4-C-5 Annex
Baltimore, MD 21235
1-800-772-1213
ssa.gov

**Society for Accessible Travel and
   Hospitality**
347 Fifth Avenue
Suite 610
New York, NY 10016
1-212-447-7284
sath.org

**Thermionics Corporation**
3501 South Sixth Street
Springfield, IL  62703
1-800-800-5728
thermipaq.com

# Index